# From the Door of the
# WHITE HOUSE

# From the Door
## of the
# WHITE HOUSE

## by Preston Bruce
With the assistance of Katharine Johnson,
Patricia Hass, and Susan Hainey

Lothrop, Lee & Shepard Books    New York

First Edition
1 2 3 4 5 6 7 8 9 10

LIBRARY OF CONGRESS CATALOGING IN PUBLICATION DATA

Bruce, Preston,
    From the door of the White House.

    Summary: A long-time White House employee recalls his many years spent serving the residents of the historical mansion.
    1. Presidents—United States—Juvenile literature. 2. White House (Washington, D.C.)—Juvenile literature. 3. Bruce, Preston, (date)—Juvenile literature. 4. Washington (D.C.)—Biography—Juvenile literature. 5. Presidents—United States—Staff—Biography—Juvenile literature. 6. Hoban, James, ca. 1762–1831—Juvenile literature. 7. Washington (D.C.)—Dwellings—Juvenile literature. [1. White House (Washington, D.C.) 2. Presidents. 3. Presidents—Staff. 4. Bruce, Preston.] I. Title.
E176.1.B895        975.3′04′0924        81-23672
ISBN 0-688-00883-6                      AACR2

7070804

# CONTENTS

# Chapter I

# EARLY MEMORIES

WHENEVER I think of my first day of work at the White House, what I remember most is seeing the mansion with Howell Crim as my guide. Howell Crim was Chief Usher. His job was to run the 123-room household, which included managing a budget of close to a million dollars and directing eighty-six household staff members—the butlers, maids, housemen, cooks, carpenters, florists, gardeners, electricians, and doormen. He kept track of the President's personal appointments, was responsible for making certain that guests were properly welcomed and made comfortable, and for keeping the house and grounds beautiful and in good working order. He had hired me to take the place of John Mays, who had retired after forty years of service as doorman.

November 15, 1953, Howell Crim spent most of the

day showing me the house that was to be the focus of my life for the next twenty-five years. I was given almost a complete tour of the mansion. We began in the Usher's Office—the nerve center of the White House living quarters and public rooms. The office was a handsome room with rich red carpet and gold draperies, though somewhat crowded with leather chairs and too many desks crammed together. There were several telephones on every desk and on the wall was a glass-covered calling board. Mr. Crim introduced me to Ushers Tom Carter and Ray Hare, two of the people with whom I would work closely in years to come, and then showed me how the calling board worked. If President or Mrs. Eisenhower pushed a buzzer upstairs, an arrow on the board would indicate who was wanted and which upstairs room he should report to.

Howell Crim walked me from room to room—from third-floor guest rooms and Solarium all the way down to the sub-basement. As we walked, he talked about the First Family, their habits, and needs, and what he felt the main purpose of a White House staff member should be. He spoke of the First Family as special and vulnerable people. To him it didn't matter what their politics were or whether you agreed with them or not. The President was elected by the people of the United States to run the country, and Howell Crim saw his job, and that of the other household staff, as helping create a place in which the President and First Lady could do their jobs well. Staff members should respect the First Family's privacy, yet be close at hand in case they needed something. We were there to do everything we could to make them comfortable and happy. He cautioned me that photographers were always around taking pictures of the President. "Help them," he said, "by staying out of the way." I understood that to mean I shouldn't shove myself into pictures with the President.

Everything he advised me that day was put in positive terms. He told me what I *should* do without saying *don't* do so and so. "If reporters ask you questions about the First Family, it isn't your job to decide how much or how little they should find out. Always tell them you don't know *any*thing."

His manner changed noticeably when we reached the upstairs family living quarters. In other parts of the house, whether in the imposing public reception rooms or in the kitchens and pantry, he was all business. But on the second floor his mood was thoughtful. He told me stories of long-gone presidents and first ladies as we walked through the Treaty Room, the Yellow Oval Room, and the Queen's Bedroom. To Mr. Crim all the first families who had once moved through these rooms were in some way still there, making their presence known. When we came to the door of the Lincoln Bedroom, he paused for a moment, then opened the door. We entered together and stood in silence.

I saw an enormous bed, seven feet long with a great black headboard eight feet high and elaborately carved. Nearby was a marble-topped table on which a small head of Lincoln rested. The expression on Lincoln's face was gentle, lonely, and sad. On another table was a glass case containing a copy of the Gettysburg Address in Lincoln's handwriting. I couldn't read the faded script.

Over the mantelpiece was a plaque on which these

words were engraved: IN THIS ROOM ABRAHAM LIN-
COLN SIGNED THE EMANCIPATION PROCLAMATION OF
JANUARY 11, 1863 WHEREBY FOUR MILLION SLAVES
WERE GIVEN THEIR FREEDOM AND SLAVERY FOREVER
PROHIBITED IN THESE UNITED STATES. My own ances-
tors were among those four million slaves. Memories of
my parents and of my boyhood washed over me as I
read those words. I remembered my father teaching
me never to forget what Abraham Lincoln did. Of all
the rooms in the White House, the Lincoln Bedroom
has always meant more to me than any other.

Here I was, Preston Bruce, forty-five years old, with
a wife and a son and daughter to support, starting a
career that was just about as far away from my beginnings in McColl, South Carolina, as could be imagined.
I was almost twenty years old when I left McColl in
June of 1928. I was a man, and my plan was to go north
and work, attend college, and make a success of my life.
I'd then return home to McColl. My father gave me
some advice the night before I left home. "Preston," he
said, "as long as you stay sober you can do whatever
anybody else can do. You've a head to think with and
two hands to work with. But remember, you're not
going to get any more than you work for. Nobody will
give you anything." He added, "Take care of what you
earn. Put it to good use. You don't have to make a lot
to be a success. The secret is to put what you earn in the
right places."

My father's advice had served me well during the
twenty-five years that had gone by since I'd left home,
and I couldn't see any reason why it wouldn't be good

for another twenty-five. My great-grandparents had come out of slavery when they were young and had taken up farming. Almost everyone in the next two generations of our family were farmers, including my father, who made his main living off the land. However, unlike many other sharecroppers, my father always had cash money in his pocket because he was also a barber in the little town of McColl. He was a good farmer and sharecropper, but it was his barber shop that made him independent.

His barber shop was a cozy place, with a pot belly stove, four big mirrors, a shiny copper kettle for hot water, and a bright electric globe. It was one of only two black-owned businesses in town. Dee Pipkin, a tailor and our great friend, had the other. Everything else in McColl was owned and run by white people. I visited my father in the shop on Saturdays. He was proud to have me there and made a big thing of introducing me to everyone who stopped by, black or white, which was something unusual for a black man to do in those days. When I was about ten, Papa gave me a shoe shine stand, and I made good with that. Then he began to teach me to barber, and by the time I was fifteen I was good enough to have a barber chair of my own. My father ordered it from Columbia, South Carolina, and it cost sixty dollars. It sat on four legs, had a drum so it could swivel and a pedal to raise or lower it.

Most of the customers in our shop were black. The exception were a few Cherokee farmers. The white people in town all went to Harrington's barber shop, which catered to whites only, though all the barbers were black. I was glad the Indians were our customers, because their hair was straight and I wanted to learn to cut all types of hair.

Our barber shop was also a focal point for the black community, and my father was like an unofficial mayor. People came to him with their problems and disputes. He tried to reason things out, and he usually succeeded. He was a peacemaker. Papa wouldn't tolerate arguments in his shop, and he encouraged good talk. Whites as well as blacks stopped by for the conversation. He called everyone who visited by name, and treated everyone with the same courtesy. I never saw him scrape or kowtow to anybody, but he never acted superior either. I'm certain my father never dreamed of how I would one day be able to make use of the lessons I learned by watching him with people in his barber shop.

I was born January 15, 1908, the oldest of seven children. My mother had a congenital heart condition and, though she wasn't sickly, she wasn't a strong woman. I remember her as very beautiful. She had long hair and large, gentle eyes. My sister Maggie was born in 1911 when I was three years old. I'd gotten used to being the kingfisher by that time, and they tell me I was pretty jealous of Maggie. My brother Russell came in 1913 and we shared a bedroom for many years. Then came Bromfield in 1915 and Fitzhugh in 1917. Dudley was born in 1919 and, last of all, came Rancy, Jr., in 1921.

We had what I thought was the biggest family in the world. Besides all my brothers and sister, my mother's two orphan brothers, Uncle Berth and Uncle Damon, lived with us. My father and my uncles and I did the heavy work on the farm, and my sister helped my mother with the younger boys and the house. My father protected my mother as best he could from the heavy demands on a farmer's wife with many children. He was the cook at breakfast time, because he wanted her to get as much rest as possible. I still remember those breakfasts. His specialty was ham and eggs, hominy grits, and biscuits, with milk fresh from the cow. Dressed and washed, the entire family sat down at the table together at sunrise.

The worst memory of my childhood is of the influenza epidemic of 1918. I've often thought that knowing we somehow made it through that time gave me the courage to think that I could endure almost any trouble. I was ten years old when it began in our area, just after Christmas. The First World War had ended and a flu virus that had started in Europe was brought to the United States by returning soldiers. There were no antibiotics to help people who developed the secondary complications of influenza then, and no vaccines to lessen its severity. Thousands of people died all over the world, including the United States.

Our schoolhouse was next door to the cemetery, and I remember sitting in school and hearing the funeral wagons rolling by. At the first sound of the crying and singing our teacher would take us all out to the graveyard to watch the people being buried. Then everything stopped—schools, churches, businesses—everything closed down. We were quarantined to try to keep the disease from spreading. People were advised to not visit one another, even to help, but they did anyway.

My mother got sick first and she was the sickest of

all our family. Then Russell, Bromfield, and Baby Fitzhugh got it. My father nearly wore himself down trying to take care of everybody, though those of us who weren't sick helped too. He kept from us news of the people we knew who had died. Later I found out about the Radly family. John Radly lived with his wife and four or five small children in a small house near us, back up in the fields. Everybody in the family died. Neighbors went in, made boxes, and put them all in the ground. They were all dead before anybody knew they were in trouble.

My father was the last to come down with the flu in our family, and that left everything up to me. The whole family was sick. I washed them all and changed their linen and tried to get nourishment into them. I fed and watered all the livestock and milked the cows. It was a complete circle around the clock. For ten days, I was the only one on my feet. Dr. Moore and Dr. Hamer stopped by and encouraged me. They said I was doing a good job. Then everyone started to get better. I still remember the relief I felt to see them sitting at the table for meals. I was the only one who didn't get sick.

My parents were determined that their children would have an education. My father wanted us to have what he didn't have, the chance to go to school. Schools for farm children in those days ran for only six months of the year. They opened in October after the bulk of the cotton was picked and ended in April or early May when the plowing and planting season began. As early as March there would be a skeleton class of mostly girls, because most of the boys had to get the land ready to seed. Sometimes I'd leave school to help with the crops, but I had a grown cousin who would plow in my place on some days until I got home at three o'clock.

Every season on the farm had its own work and rewards. After plowing and fertilizing, it was time to plant. You had to throw two little rows together and build a furrow. Then you followed the work horse who pulled a machine that would drop the seed. In a couple of weeks you'd see the little green shoots. Then we had the problem of thinning it all out, so the plants would be six inches apart. Cotton comes up very thick; we'd have to chop it out by hand, with a hoe. Later you'd have to pick out the grass, so it wouldn't take over. My father could hire people for seventy-five cents a day to do the chopping and weeding if there was more than we could do.

On Saturday nights I stayed late at the barber shop with my father until midnight when the shop closed. We talked together as we drove home. On one of those nights when I was about seventeen, my father announced that he didn't want me to be a "cotton boy" all my life. "That's no future for you," he said. "The boll weevil is taking the future out of it for all of us." The boll weevil is a small, hard insect that punctures the tough cotton boll and eats out the inside before the cotton can form. Despite the use of insecticides, we were getting less than a bale of cotton per acre instead of the two bales we used to get.

"Well, there's tobacco," I said. "Lots of people are switching to tobacco for a money crop."

"I may do that," my father answered, "but it won't be easy for people like us to go into tobacco. Your opportunities are too limited here. Education is the only way for our people. This fall I'm sending you to Laurinburg Institute. You need more education than you can get around here."

I was prompted to ask a question that had been bothering me a long time.

"Papa, why is it that our work tending crops enables white people to enjoy so many luxuries? How did Mr. Tatum get to own thousands of acres of land, and we can't even go into the places that our work makes him able to afford?"

"It all comes straight out of slavery, Preston. Mr. Tatum, Mr. Fletcher, and all the others inherited their land and status. It's unequal, Preston, but it's not completely without hope for us. I have a cousin, Caroline Breedon, whose forebear was given land by a white man after he was freed from slavery by Abraham Lincoln. That family has that land to this day."

"I've heard it said that Abraham Lincoln didn't care that much about black people," I said.

Papa answered, "Lincoln is the one who emancipated us. I have to believe the man at heart." Then he fixed me with a stern eye and said, "Preston, judge a man by the deed he does, not by his race or place in life."

Then he continued, "Abraham Lincoln was a Republican. One day you'll vote, and when that day comes I hope you'll vote Republican."

I have often wondered how my father could have had such faith that I would vote someday. He had never voted. He had never been allowed to. Yet he had faith that in my future black people would gain the vote, and that having a voice in the way our country is governed would make a difference in the way black people could live their lives.

And so he'd seen to it that I was as educated as he could possibly afford and, when the time came, encouraged me to leave home. I was less than twenty when I went to Washington D.C., and forty-five when I went to work at the White House. Those twenty-five years in between were important preparation for the next twenty-five.

My first job for the government was as an assistant laborer in the Treasury-Federal Warehouse. For a forty-hour week, I was paid thirty-five dollars every two weeks, no sick leave, no medical insurance. I gradually moved up the ladder: from stockroom assistant to assistant messenger in the mailroom. During World War II, the army wouldn't have me because of a heart murmur. I was promoted to head messenger for the District Engineer's Office, which was in charge of building the Pentagon. By the end of the war, I was in charge of a department of fifteen people. I came to my job at the White House with a lot of experience working with and managing people, organizing, and making the most of opportunities when they presented themselves.

When the opportunity to work at the White House came, my first reaction was that the title "doorman" sounded as though the job would involve nothing more than opening doors. Since I knew the job involved more than that, I decided to ignore how it might sound to other people. I was excited at the idea that I would be working with the President of the United States.

# Chapter 2

# THE EISENHOWERS

IT was my second day at the White House that I met Mamie Eisenhower. Mr. Crim explained as he took me upstairs that Mrs. Eisenhower was a very systematic woman. She liked to work in bed in the mornings, and I would be bringing her mail and packages to her bedroom each morning. If her door was ajar it meant she was ready to begin her day. If it was closed, I should not disturb her.

When we entered the room, Mrs. Eisenhower was sitting up in bed with a lap desk over her knees. She was wearing a lacy dressing gown and had a pink ribbon in her hair. A secretary was sitting next to the bed poised to take dictation as Mrs. Eisenhower went through the stacks of mail surrounding her. At that very moment, Mrs. Eisenhower was having a brisk conversation with Maître D' Charles Ficklen about an upcoming formal dinner. It was obvious that the frilly-looking bedroom was a command post. It was also clear that Mrs. Eisenhower was an experienced executive who ran a tight ship.

With a big smile that lit up her whole face, Mamie Eisenhower gave me a warm welcome. "Bruce," she said, "we will be calling on you a lot." Then to Mr. Crim, she said, "I want Ike to meet Bruce soon." She made me feel that she really wanted me at the White House. Her manner was that welcoming.

The next day I met the President. I was eager to meet him, but I was also very nervous. Mr. Crim and I were waiting in the ground-floor hallway for the President to leave the Oval Office for his lunch. The door at the end of the long corridor opened, and out bounced Mr. Eisenhower, his Secret Service detail trotting fast to keep up with him.

I saw a tall, trim man with the straight back and erect shoulders of a soldier. He wore a dark brown suit and brightly striped tie. He was nearly bald, but his quick step and the lively expression on his smooth face were youthful.

The President spotted us standing there and he called out, "Hi, Mr. Crim, who have we got here?" So Mr. Crim introduced me. The President told me he was glad to have me aboard. He was friendly, but I could feel him looking me over. I noticed his square, stubborn chin. I'd heard of his quick temper.

I took the President to the second floor and as he got out of the elevator he turned to me and, for the first time, I saw General Ike's gorgeous grin that had endeared him to millions during World War II. "I hope you're going to be happy here, Bruce," he said.

* * *

There was just one place Mr. Crim didn't personally take me on our tour of the White House, though it was a place I'd be visiting every day with Mrs. Eisenhower's packages and mail. That was the Social Office, down on the ground floor, where the First Lady's Social Secretary, Mary Jane McCaffery, held sway. James Harriston took me over to the East Wing and introduced me to Miss McCaffery and her assistants.

I soon understood why Mr. Crim didn't escort me to the Social Office. That was not his territory. The Chief Usher of the White House has absolute authority over the household employees, some of whom have worked there for twenty or thirty or more years, under many different presidents and first ladies. The staff are the people who stay on, who know all the ins and outs of how to run the White House.

But the Social Office people all come in new with each First Lady. She hires her own Social Secretary who reports directly to her. Each Social Secretary has to start from scratch learning the ropes.

So the Chief Usher and the Social Secretary each has his or her own kingdom, but their functions overlap so naturally there is tension. I watched Mr. Crim and Miss McCaffery, and I saw that neither could push the other too hard. They worked together. They had to.

In those very first days I saw that there was something I could do for Mrs. Eisenhower that was much more important than carrying her mail and packages back and forth to the Social Office—that was to take care of her friends.

Mamie Eisenhower was a sociable person. She had

her duties to perform as the President's wife, and she performed them like the soldier's wife she was. But she also took time for her friends. She was the only First Lady while I was at the White House who did that. The staff liked the idea of the First Lady having her friends for lunch and card games once a week. She needed that. A First Lady's life shouldn't be strictly business seven days a week, but that was the way it was for the other presidents' wives who followed Mrs. Eisenhower.

The first thing I did when I got to the White House was to take care of guests in my own way, and I started with Mrs. Eisenhower's friends. I decided to give every guest special attention. My job made me the first person someone coming into the White House would meet, and I believed that whether you're big or small, you're important once you're invited there. I felt it was up to me to show the dignity, the grace, the formality of the White House, in my greeting.

First I studied the list of guests expected. Each person has a *name* and I decided that I must know it. I decided it was my business to help the visitors relax. I realized that just about everyone who comes to the White House is excited and nervous. Some are scared stiff. The big person, like an ambassador or a senator who has an appointment with the President, may well have the same butterflies in his stomach as a maid coming to interview for a job. I treated all visitors alike. I greeted them by name and talked comfortably with them. It gave them time to compose themselves. I can talk to anyone. I learned that from my father.

So when Mrs. Gruenther and Mrs. Titus and Mrs. Allen came to visit the First Lady, I knew their names, and if they had to wait, I'd pass the time of day and chat with them. Like Mrs. Eisenhower, they were outgoing and friendly—they almost seemed like sisters together —and they liked the way I welcomed them. It was something new. They told Mrs. Eisenhower that I had made them feel right at home.

Mrs. Eisenhower was delighted and that was how our close relationship began.

Within my first two weeks on the job, I saw the White House in full action at a formal dinner. It was for the Justices of the Supreme Court. I could feel the tension starting two days before the dinner as Ben Harrison and the other housemen started an orgy of cleaning. They knew Mrs. Eisenhower's eagle eye would spot a speck of dust or a fingerprint, and they weren't anxious to displease her.

By noon of the day of the dinner, after the usual thousand or more tourists had finished trooping through the White House on the morning tour, the entire staff went into high gear. Whenever I could, I snatched the time to watch the transformation of the State Dining Room.

I greatly admired Charles Ficklen, the stately maître d'. He was the chief architect of the entire event—like the conductor of a symphony orchestra, he directed the thirty butlers, the five pantry girls, the seven carpenters, the four electricians, the chef and several cooks, the seven or eight housemen, and a number of florists, all of whom had to dovetail their work. This staff was a mixture of White House regulars—and most of us worked a double shift on that day—and outside help, many of whom had been coming for White House dinners for twenty years or more.

Up from the basement on one small freight elevator came heavy wooden crates containing the eight hundred pieces of china, four hundred glasses, and eight hundred pieces of gold knives, forks, and spoons to be used at the dinner. There is no room to store all of this on the first floor of the White House, which was designed to be a beautiful home for presidents, not a place for huge functions. The early presidents never dreamed of having the big dinners that are held there today.

While all this equipment was being unloaded, the carpenters were setting up the big u-shaped table that President and Mrs. Eisenhower liked. They always sat in the "u" where they could look in the faces of each one of their guests. That way, every guest would feel he was having dinner with the President and First Lady.

While the butlers fanned out around the State Dining Room with linen, china, and glass, Mr. Redmon, the florist, and his assistants brought in the flower arrangements they'd labored over since the early hours of the morning.

Everyone was working at top speed. What impressed me most was the teamwork and the timing. I felt as if I were in a theater, and on the stage every player was a professional who knew his part, letter perfect. No one made a wasted motion or a mistake. Even so, the tension mounted. You could feel it in the air. Tempers flared.

The Usher's Office was headquarters. It wasn't big enough, and the phones all rang at once. Too many people needed to be coming in and out. Mr. Crim was on hand to make instant decisions, and he didn't enjoy working in such crowded conditions. Finally he exploded, "There's not enough room in here to skin a cat!"

At six o'clock I brought Mrs. Eisenhower down from the second floor to look over the dining room. She was gracious and charming as she admired everything and told Mr. Ficklen and Mr. Crim what a fine job everyone had done. Her visit helped everyone to simmer down.

The Marine Band arrived in their scarlet uniforms to set up their instruments in the lobby. They started to play just before the first group of guests, the honored dignitaries, arrived. James Harriston and I met the guests and took them upstairs to visit with the President and First Lady before dinner.

At the stroke of eight the main body of guests started to pour into the North Lobby. Suddenly that space, which seemed so vast when empty, completely filled up with people. And despite all the staff on duty, we were short-handed.

I helped the guests with their coats, then young military aides in full dress uniform escorted them over to a table, placed near the band, where James Wade, another doorman, was standing. The table was piled with hand-lettered white cards and envelopes. On each envelope was the name of a guest, and inside was a diagram of the dining table showing where that guest was supposed to sit. Then there was another card with the guest's name on it for a military aide to pick up. The aide would escort the guest to the East Room and announce his name to the President and First Lady.

The idea was to make every guest of the President feel special, even though he or she was part of a large group. However, it was quickly apparent that the system wasn't working the way it was supposed to.

The music was so loud that guests had to shout their names into the ears of the aides who had to pick up their cards. The aides, bending down over the low table, had trouble reading the cards that were turned the wrong way around. There were too many cards and envelopes for the small table, and some were falling on the floor. Some guests didn't get the right cards and were milling around the dining room, not knowing where to sit. There were only three mix-ups, but that was three too many. I decided right then that I wanted to improve on this part of a formal dinner, but I was too new to suggest changes and right then wasn't the right moment anyway.

As the last guests got their cards and were escorted to the receiving line, the Marine Band struck up "Ruffles and Flourishes" and then "Hail to the Chief." The noisy lobby quieted and every eye turned to the main staircase. First came the Honor Guard, led by two soldiers carrying the American and presidential flags— each flagpole had a golden eagle at the top. All the men were in full dress uniform with loops of gold braid over their shoulders, white-gloved hands clenched at their sides.

Then came the President and First Lady. Dwight D. Eisenhower in the tuxedo he hated and a bejeweled Mamie Eisenhower in a full-skirted satin evening gown.

After every guest had moved through the receiving line to shake hands with the Eisenhowers, they had to be moved quickly into the State Dining Room. Tom Carter told me that once the President was seated, we had to close the doors. Latecomers would get *no* dinner. Those were the President's orders. He kept no one waiting, and he'd wait for no man.

The way the food got to all eighty-odd guests piping hot was a miracle. Pearl Wiggins and her assistants in the pantry had beautifully arranged the hot food on big silver serving trays. They had to work *fast* in very close, hot quarters. Then the butlers, under Eugene Allen, moved the trays into the dining room like soldiers in a close-order drill.

While the guests were eating, I went into the East Room to put out the tassled programs on the gold chairs that had been set up for the musicale after dinner. I then came back into the State Dining Room for the toasts, standing in the back with Tom Carter and James Wade.

The room hushed as the President raised his glass. It was the high point of the evening for me. I could hardly believe that I was here, in this room, with the President of the United States. I felt as if I were in a dream: flowers, dresses, china, silver, candles on the table, and chandeliers above, all melted into a sea of colors, soft and bright.

Behind the President was a somber portrait of Abraham Lincoln hung over the mantelpiece. A brass plate on the mantelpiece had these words engraved on it:

*The White House Blessing*
I pray heaven to bestow the best of blessings on This
    House
And on all that shall hereafter inhabit it
May none but honest and wise men rule under this roof.
John Quincy Adams
First President to live in the White House

It was getting late. I'd been at the White House since six-thirty that morning, as had many others, but there was more work for all of us.

After dinner the women guests moved with Mrs. Eisenhower into the Red Room for coffee. There were plenty of chairs and sofas, but no one sat down because the First Lady was standing. That was the rule. I stood in the doorway with one of the Secret Service men. Then I spotted something astonishing.

One of the well-dressed ladies had been stirring her coffee with a tiny gold spoon. She gave a quick look around, opened her brocaded evening bag, and popped in the spoon. Click, the bag snapped shut. Nobody saw it but me.

I spoke quietly to one of the Secret Service men, but he frowned and motioned me out into the hall, where he told me there was nothing to be done about the lady who stole the spoon. It was very important to the President that this dinner go smoothly, and it would be awkward and embarrassing to the other guests to confront the thief. It was hard for me to accept this then, and I never did get used to it, though I was to learn later that it happened all the time. Some people managed to take even the doorknobs! To me, everything in the White House is a part of history. The House and everything in it belongs to all Americans, a treasure to be handed down from one generation to the next.

Mrs. Eisenhower allowed her guests to smoke cigarettes with their coffee, but there was absolutely no smoking allowed in the East Room, with its gold velvet-smooth carpet. I was posted at the door of the East Room with an oversized ashtray to catch the guests as they filed past and persuade them to give me their cigars and cigarettes. I discovered I had to be tactful but firm. People didn't want to stop smoking. However, they had to, because the First Lady said so.

After the musicale, I took the President and Mrs. Eisenhower upstairs. That was the signal for the guests to leave. Then it was my job to secure the second floor after the President and First Lady went to bed.

When I came downstairs about midnight, J. B. West told me I could go home. The butlers and others still had work to do. I was very tired. But I was happy too. I'd seen the White House at its most beautiful, and the staff, like a well-oiled machine, doing a great job. I felt good to be part of the team. I'd begun to settle in.

Dwight D. Eisenhower was a private person. I admired him as I watched him with his aides. You can tell a lot about a person from the sort of people he hires and the way he treats them. The two people closest to President Eisenhower, outside of his family, were Governor Sherman Adams, his most powerful and trusted aide in the Oval Office, and John Moaney, his valet.

Governor Adams was known around the White House as "the little man with ice water in his veins." He reminded you of the long, cold winters of his native New Hampshire. The President depended on him completely. He was his Chief of Staff.

Sherman Adams was a spare, gray-haired man who rarely smiled. He arrived for work at 6:30 A.M., and as late as 10:00 P.M., I'd see his Oldsmobile still parked on the circular drive near the Oval Office. His manner was abrupt, his words were few. Yet when the President introduced me to him, I instantly trusted and respected him and felt he returned the respect. A lot of people were afraid of him, and if you were not up to his standards, you had reason to be, but if you were a conscientious and honest person, then you were all right in his book.

There was a contrast between the President's regard for Sherman Adams and the way he felt about Richard Nixon, his Vice-President. Governor Adams was a frequent visitor to the second floor—he was like a member of the family. The Vice-President, however, was never invited there except when there was an official party.

John Moaney, the President's valet, had been with General and Commander-in-Chief Eisenhower as his mess sergeant all through World War II. Moaney was a full-faced brown-skinned man with sandy hair that was beginning to go gray. He dressed casually in neat slacks, sport shirt, and a cardigan sweater or jacket. With his wife Dolores, who worked for Mrs. Eisenhower, Moaney lived in the White House and was on call night and day. Wherever the President went, Moaney went too. Moaney was so attached to the President he refused to take a day off. No one could attend to the President but John. His position was absolutely secure and he wasn't a bit afraid of his boss.

I enjoyed going to the third floor to talk with John while he was doing the President's laundry. He thought nothing of ironing twenty-seven shirts at a clip and as many undershorts.

What I liked best was the relationship between these two men—Ike and his mess sergeant. Every morning at seven sharp I'd bring the elevator up to the second floor to collect the President and take him downstairs to the office. I'd wait in the hall outside the President's bedroom where he was dressing, and through the door I'd hear hilarious laughter between the President and John Moaney. No one in the White House ever knew what jokes they shared. Suddenly the President's door would open. Out John would step, his face so pokered it looked as though he never smiled. As the President stepped across the threshold, he stuck out his arm and Moaney would deftly slide a watch over his wrist. The President never missed a step. That was a daily routine they'd polished.

Moaney would work too long without a break. Day in, day out, he'd never go outside. Finally the pressure would get to him and he'd start to taste gin, and then he couldn't stop. He couldn't stand being cooped up in the White House any longer. The President understood the problem and would urge John to take time off. But John wouldn't do it, because he was afraid someone else might get too close to the President while he was away.

When John was drinking, the President would get furious with him, but he'd protect him, too. He'd tell everyone—the Secret Service, even Mrs. Eisenhower—"I'll be responsible for what John does." Once or twice a year he'd have to force John to take two or three days off, and while John was away, the President had to take care of himself because Moaney had carefully not told anybody else what to do for him.

When John came back to the White House, he'd be sober as a judge, but the President would still be mad. John would pull out a suit for the President to wear; the President would ignore that suit and pull another one out of the closet. He wouldn't even speak to John for a day or two. Then he'd get over it and soon they'd be back together just as before. They were inseparable.

I watched President Eisenhower inside the White House and I paid close attention to his actions. I wondered if he would make good on his campaign promise to rid Washington, D.C. of segregation, to make it a "show place" for the rest of the nation.

At that time, Washington, D.C. was just another southern town. I had tried to rise above it. Our family didn't care to go to the stores, theaters, or restaurants where we weren't welcome. But there was no way you could forget segregation. All the D.C. newspapers, for instance, completely blanked out the black community. In the District of Columbia, we had to read the Baltimore *Afro-American* or the Pittsburgh *Courier,* both black-owned papers, to find out what our own black leaders were saying.

I remember a trip to South Carolina by train. At Union Station, in Washington, D.C., I'd have to get on one car alone—number 11E. Every black person who wanted to go south had to cram into that car, which was sandwiched between the engine, with its coal chutes, and the baggage car. We were trapped in there, overcrowded, standing and sitting in the aisles, though there were plenty of seats on the rest of the train. Elbows in each other's way, we ate food we had brought with us because we couldn't go to the diner.

Going through a tunnel, the noise from the engine next to us was unbelievable. You nearly choked on the coal dust—it would stay in your throat for hours—and you could almost cough up soot. That horrible trip took twelve hours. I never will forget it.

In November of 1953 change was in the air. The Supreme Court was in the process of deciding *Brown* v. *Board of Education*—one of the most important cases of this century. The judges had to decide whether or not segregated schools were unconstitutional.

*"Brown"*—was Linda Carol Brown, eight years old, who wasn't allowed to go to the white elementary school four blocks from her home in Topeka, Kansas. Instead, Linda had to attend an inferior school for black children, twenty blocks away, across a dangerous railroad bridge.

I waited anxiously for the outcome of this case. My daughter Elaine was training to be a teacher, and I wanted her and my future grandchildren to come into an open public school system. Just weeks after I started work at the White House, the nine justices listened to oral arguments in the *Brown* case. In the black-owned papers I read of the courtroom drama.

The Supreme Court chambers were packed to overflowing. To speak for segregated schools was the famous eighty-two-year-old former Democratic Presidential candidate John W. Davis, dressed in formal morning coat. To speak for Linda Carol Brown, President Eisenhower's Attorney General, Herbert Brownell, sent a young black attorney dressed in a business suit. His name was Thurgood Marshall and today he is the first black Justice of the Supreme Court of the United States.

The arguments climaxed in an emotional exchange. First John W. Davis sneered that all this case meant was that Negroes were trying to acquire "prestige."

"Exactly correct," Thurgood Marshall shouted. "Ever since Emancipation, Negroes have been trying to get the same status as everybody else."

The judges had to ponder their decision, so it was some months before the outcome was known. But segregation in my hometown was about to end, because

Dwight D. Eisenhower, as President of the United States, was the boss in the District of Columbia. He didn't have to wait for the Supreme Court decision to make changes there.

One day I looked at the schedule of visitors in the Usher's Office and saw a name that amazed me: the Elder Michaux. This colorful personage was famous in the black community, but he was almost unknown to the white people of Washington.

Elder "Lightfoot" Michaux was the pastor of a large congregation at his Church of God on Georgia Avenue. He was known as the "Happy Am I" preacher, from the song he sang on his daily radio program, which was broadcast from coast to coast. He ran the Happy News Cafe, where for a penny a meal he fed the hungry and housed the homeless.

Usher West told me, "Bruce, Elder Michaux and the President will have lunch together on trays upstairs in the West Hall. This visit is *strictly* off-the-record. Don't say a word of it to anyone."

I was astonished. Publicity was to the Elder Michaux like mother's milk. He was a showman. He baptized huge crowds of people at Griffith's Stadium using water from the River Jordan, backed by massed choirs and marching bands. The idea of Reverend Michaux passing up the chance to publicize his meeting with the President of the United States was hard to believe.

Also, President Eisenhower only ordered lunch on trays upstairs for his closest aides and his personal friends. He'd hold stag luncheons in the Family Dining Room downstairs to talk business, but upstairs was where he relaxed.

I was pleased to greet Elder Michaux and escort him

to the President. The tall, elegant preacher hummed his way upstairs in the elevator. In the West Hall, the President and the pastor, arms around each other, patting each other on the back, greeted each other like old friends. Later I learned that back before the war, the then Major Eisenhower had been made an honorary deacon of the Church of God by the Elder Michaux.

The President had asked me to stay nearby, and I was fascinated with their conversation as they sat side by side on a flowered sofa.

Pastor Michaux described to President Eisenhower how angry and impatient black people were feeling, and he asked, point-blank, what was the President going to do to help?

The President replied that he was going to put the heat on the D.C. commissioners, whom he had appointed to their jobs, to carry out his executive order to desegregate restaurants, theaters, and other public places in the District. He was fed up, he said, with the commissioners dragging their feet about following his orders. He would force them to act by using all the power he had, behind the scenes. Then he would let them take the credit.

The Elder Michaux liked the President's plan and gave him tips about how to carry it out. It was clear that Elder Michaux was a vital pipeline into the D.C. black community. During many such secret meetings between these two men, I watched President Eisenhower work to improve race relations in D.C. and beyond.

There were those who criticized the President because they thought he moved too *slowly* on racial issues, but I had friends in South Carolina who feared he

34

was moving too *fast*—that it was dangerous to integrate the races. Black people in the South lived under a constant threat of violence.

I well understood the fears of black southerners because I too grew up under the threat of violence. Our family adapted to it as best we could, without much bitterness, because my father was such a serious Christian, he wouldn't judge all white people by the brutal actions of some.

In our little town of McColl, the white workers from the cotton mill were overworked, ill-paid, and rough. They had come from poor, hard-scrabble hill country leaving their roots behind. They took out their anger and frustrations on black people.

One Sunday afternoon when my father and I were driving home from church together in the buggy, an old car filled with drunken white mill hands came up behind us on the road. They stuck their guns out of the car windows and started shooting at us and under the hooves of our horse, Molly. They made their car backfire and tried to force us off the road. I thought they were going to shoot the horse or shoot my father.

The poor horse screamed, jumped, and reared; my father barely kept the buggy from overturning. The gang followed us as Molly galloped toward home which, luckily, was nearby.

My father drove the buggy into our yard, jumped out, and ran into the house to get his 30-30 rifle, while my Uncle Damon caught the horse's reins. Mama hung onto Papa, begging him not to go back outside where the mill workers were waiting.

Our landowner, Will Seals, heard the shooting and

brought four or five men to the rescue. Armed with rifles and pistols, they made citizens' arrests and took the mill hands to the police.

These men didn't know my father or me. They thought it was fun to frighten a black man and his son.

When I was an older boy, my father kept me under severe restrictions for my safety. I had to be home at sundown; I couldn't stand around the street corners in town with my friends; I could never carry a gun.

Papa trusted me to stay out of trouble, but at that time in the South, the police would pull a young black man into jail for nothing—for "looking suspicious." It was their method for keeping young blacks in line, to nip in the bud any possible protest against rigid segregation. As I look back, it's a miracle that out of six boys, not one of us was ever in jail.

Even worse than the police, gangs of young white mill hands would be out after dark looking for black boys to beat up, sometimes horribly. And they amused themselves wrecking the cars of black people. No one ever seemed to know who did these things or why.

My experience of growing up in the South caused me to agree with the President's middle-of-the-road approach on race. He kept the pressure on, behind the scenes, but he wouldn't attack segregationists publicly to humiliate them, because he believed he wouldn't get results that way. He didn't want to inflame ugly passions, endangering innocent people.

I was encouraged as the system of segregation began to unravel, under President Eisenhower's lead. I remember my first trip south on a desegregated train. From the White House I phoned for a reserved seat to Hamlet, North Carolina, and another one back to Washington. No one asked me if I were black or white. I went to Union Station and I picked up my reservation; no problem. Not a soul hassled me all the way to Hamlet.

But when my visit was over and I got back on the train in Hamlet to return to Washington, the conductor looked at my ticket and said, "You are supposed to go to car 11E."

"*No,*" I answered. "I am supposed to get in *this* coach. This is my seat. I am supposed to have it."

I intended to stay in that seat or I was going to get the conductor's name in order to sue him and the railroad. So rather than face a suit, the conductor let me stay in the seat I had reserved and paid for.

I rode all the way back to Washington in the coach at the rear of the train, so far away from car 11E up next to the engine. I had a young white girl as my seatmate. We exchanged magazines and we napped. It was a fine trip.

The Supreme Court decided *Brown* v. *Board of Education* in favor of Linda Carol Brown. My daughter Elaine was given her first teaching assignment, an appointment to an all-white school that had never before had a black teacher or a black student. She had a fantastic year in that school—the principal and her pupils loved her.

I also saw the President tackle Congress. I was proud to usher into the White House men such as Speaker Sam Rayburn of Texas, Senator Everett Dirksen of Illinois, Senator George of Georgia, and others whose support the President was seeking for the first Civil Rights Bill, since 1875, to ensure the basic right of black people to *vote.*

The President invited to these meetings men he knew were on his side, and he also asked some who were on the fence but seemed open-minded. He *never* invited rock-ribbed white supremacy advocates, like Senator Harold Stennis of Mississippi, or Rules Committee Chairman "Judge" Smith of Virginia.

Upstairs in the Yellow Oval Room, time and again, I'd hear the President say, "I want you people to go back to Capitol Hill and back to your home states and tell everyone who will listen to you sensibly that *these injustices have to be corrected.* Nobody is going to ram anything down their throats, but the United States must lead the world and set a good example. You must get people to change their minds and hearts. I want this bill passed, and I won't let Congress leave for the year until something satisfactory is done."

These meetings *never* hit the papers. The newsmen never knew these strategy sessions took place in the White House. No one has ever told of them as far as I know. But I was *there.*

That bill did pass, finally, in 1954.

President Eisenhower set goals he felt he could meet. Unlike most politicians, he wouldn't go out on the stump and make a lot of promises he couldn't keep. He wasn't worried about what people were going to think or say about him, but he was extremely worried about violence. He wanted to see justice done, but he also wanted to keep the country calm. He wouldn't grandstand on TV, lest he inflame hotheads and cause innocent people to get hurt. There were people on the extremes of both sides, black and white, who were just looking for an excuse to start riots. It was a tinderbox situation.

Despite the round-the-clock pressures of his office, President Eisenhower knew how to relax. I liked to see him do that.

One White House privilege the Eisenhowers loved was the movie theater. They could ask for any movie and immediately it would be flown in from California. The White House theater has full cinemascope and seats a hundred. The First Family invited whomever they chose to watch movies with them, while the butlers stood ready to serve drinks and refreshments in the theater.

Ike would watch two westerns at a sitting, but he disliked gangster films. Certain actors he loved—others he hated and would stamp out of the theater in a temper if their faces showed up on the screen. I always stayed in the theater with the President to answer the telephone—a disagreeable job since Mr. Eisenhower hated to be interrupted in the middle of a movie. I'd ask the caller his name. If it was somebody very high up, like a cabinet officer, I'd bring the phone by its fifteen-foot cord to the President at his seat. Otherwise I'd say, "The President is watching a movie, do you want to interrupt him?" Let *him* catch the heat, I thought.

President Eisenhower enjoyed the friendship of many powerful, successful businessmen. Once a month, he'd invite five or six of these men for a weekend of bridge playing, joking, and relaxing on the second floor of the White House.

One of these friends was big and jovial, a top man at City Service Oil Corporation. I didn't mind hanging up his beautiful suits to help out John Moaney, who was busy with other guests. I also helped him arrange to get back to the private plane that would take him to New York on Sunday evenings.

Moaney and I and the other household staff liked these jolly weekend parties. These guests were not demanding. They were glad to have informal dinners on trays with the President and First Lady. These weekends always did the President good, and by Sunday evenings his worry lines were gone.

One Sunday evening, as I was helping the friendly oil magnate pack his suitcase, he suddenly asked me how I would like to have a City Service credit card.

I smiled and answered, "I try to avoid credit cards. I like to stay out of debt."

His reply was smooth. "Well, Bruce, you wouldn't get the bills. Those bills would come to me, and I'd take care of them."

Instantly into my mind flashed pictures of the wonderful places I could take my family on all that free gasoline. I pushed away those enticing thoughts and said to the oilman that I'd have to think it over.

I told the whole story to J. B. West, who was Chief Usher at the time.

J.B. said, "Bruce, you were wise to tell me about this. I'm sure the President's guest was just being thoughtful and meant you no harm. But it is strictly against White House rules for any employee to take expensive gifts from anyone he meets here. You might have been asked for inside information or some other improper favor in exchange for the free gas."

That credit card, had I accepted it, would have cost me my job. I guess I'll never know if the executive intended to ask me for improper favors as payment for the free gas. I hope not.

\*   \*   \*

The President liked to cook his famous mulligan stew for his friends. Ike and Mr. Moaney would disappear up to the third floor kitchen on Saturday afternoons, and soon the whole White House would smell of browning meat, gobs of garlic, onions, and spices. When the proud chefs produced their concoction, there was enough for the whole staff for lunch as well as the guests. And it was delicious!

The President was an avid golfer. On sunny afternoons he'd tap away on his putting green on the White House lawn, his golfing cap stuck rakishly over one ear. One afternoon I saw him in his golfing clothes sneaking into the East Room where the First Lady was greeting a group of boy scouts from Nebraska. He wanted to say hello, but he was banished by his wife. She disapproved of his costume.

On Saturdays the President liked to paint at his easel in his studio on the second floor. He didn't mind if I stood quietly by and watched him. When he was pleased with something he'd done, the President had his pictures reproduced as Christmas presents for all of us on the White House staff.

The most important way the President relaxed was with his family. The Eisenhowers were very close. Every day, the President hurried back from the Oval Office to be strictly on time for one o'clock lunch and seven o'clock dinner with "my Mamie." The First Lady insisted that the President have regular meals. Mrs. Eisenhower had no interest in politics, but she cared a lot about people and was a shrewd judge of them. She could spot insincerity right away. I often heard the

President ask for her opinion of somebody, and he always listened carefully to her answer.

The Eisenhowers loved their grandchildren and invited them for long visits. Their tricycles and wagons were always welcome. When I first came to the White House there was David, Barbara Ann, and Susan, aged six, four, and two. Then little Mary Jean was born, and I watched her christening in the Blue Room.

David and the President went to church together regularly, David in his bow tie standing straight beside his grandfather. One Sunday, Mrs. Eisenhower called me to the second floor. The President and David were late for lunch, and I must go up to the third floor to see what they were doing.

I heard two excited voices as I approached the big sunny room. There was the President, down on his hands and knees with David who was laying out his toy soldiers. David finished arranging his troops.

"No! No!" shouted General Ike. "That's all wrong! Their left flank is exposed!" With a sweep of his hand, the President knocked down David's soldiers. David had to rearrange them with their flanks properly protected before the two would come downstairs to Sunday lunch.

Mrs. Eisenhower went all out for Christmas. The White House was festooned from top to bottom. The white columns were looped with garlands, holly tied with bows of red ribbon hung from the chandeliers. There were wreaths around the candlesticks and bright red poinsettias and other flowers everywhere.

The first time the grandchildren spent Christmas at the White House, I counted eleven different trees. On the first floor, there was the huge blue spruce, which took six men to drag in and set up. For three days, ten or twelve people at a time would take time off from their regular jobs to trim the tree with ornaments, toy soldiers, flutes, drums, flowers, and sugarplum fairies.

There were seven more decorated trees on the first floor, two outside the North Door and another large one in the Oval Study on the second floor where the President kept his war trophies, such as the gold sword trimmed with pearls given him by the Queen of Holland. On the third floor there was a little balsam pine for David and his sisters.

While she was decorating the White House, Mrs. Eisenhower was buying and wrapping hundreds of presents—not just for those of us who worked at the White House, but for our families too. She wrote a card to go with each present. For me, she selected some fine cuff links and toys for the children.

On Christmas day, the Eisenhowers went to church and then opened their gifts. It tickled me to watch the President. He was like a small boy, so pleased with his presents. Then the family had early Christmas dinner, and I went home to enjoy Christmas with my own family.

Despite all the President's efforts to unwind, he lived in a pressure cooker. Sometimes his temper showed it. He kept to a split-second schedule and never, ever kept anyone waiting. What he couldn't stand was to be kept waiting himself.

My particular worry was the elevator to the second floor. It developed a bad habit—the lock would stick if I put it on hold. I had told the electrician about it several times, but he hadn't gotten around to fixing it. I lived in fear that one day I wouldn't have the elevator when the President wanted it, and he'd have to wait.

Most mornings, Colonel Robert Schultz, the President's senior military aide, liked to ride upstairs with me in the elevator and travel back down with the President. Colonel Schultz took care of the President's personal finances and made all his travel arrangements. He was a kind man, who wanted everything to go as smooth as silk for his boss, and got very upset when anything went wrong. On the way upstairs one morning, I told Colonel Schultz about the elevator's bad habit. He turned pale.

"You know the President can't stand to waste one minute," he said, as if the balky elevator was my fault.

"I certainly hope he won't have to," I replied.

We arrived at the second floor and stepped out of the elevator. I did not dare to lock it in case I couldn't get it to move again.

Colonel Schultz and I stood waiting in the hallway. We could see the light under the President's bedroom door. Then I heard the sound I'd been dreading—softly the elevator doors glided shut—the elevator was gone!

At that very moment, the bedroom door opened, and President Eisenhower saw that the elevator door was closed. His face darkened. He was ready to begin his day and now he was stopped dead in his tracks.

"Bruce," he snapped, "*where* is the elevator?"

"I'm very sorry, Mr. President," I explained. "Someone has called it. I can't put it on hold, because the lock sticks."

I kept my finger on the elevator button to call it back up to the second floor.

The President waited silently for about one minute, then he began to boil. Hand on hip, brow wrinkled, he began to tap his foot on the floor as he watched the dial. The elevator went down to the basement, then back to the first floor, where it stopped. He was angrier than I'd ever seen him. He seemed eight feet tall.

Colonel Schultz panicked and began to pace up and down the long hall. His natty military cap sat askew on his head, and his moustache quivered. He wrung his hands and cried, "Run and catch the elevator, Bruce! Go downstairs and bring it back!"

Colonel Schultz wanted to help, but he was making the President more tense. He was making it harder for me too.

I explained to him, "That will just waste more time. As long as I keep my finger on the button, the elevator has to return."

In the meantime, John Moaney stood by the bedroom door, watching quietly, a tiny flicker of amusement showing at the corners of his mouth. He was curious to see what would happen.

The elevator returned. The whole event took maybe five minutes, but it seemed like an hour.

The angry President, Colonel Schultz, and I rode in silence to the first floor. I wasn't about to apologize.

Just as the President was leaving, I did speak up.

"I'm terribly sorry that this happened, Mr. President. This elevator sticks and will not move after it has been locked on hold."

The President barked, "Well, what's wrong? Does it need something done to it?"

"It needs repairing. I regret you were held up this morning," I answered.

The President began to calm down.

"That's all right, Bruce. It's not your fault. But you go

back and tell Mr. West that if he can't get this elevator fixed, take the damn thing out and put in a new one!" Within two days all new works were put into the elevator. It has worked perfectly ever since.

As the President approached the end of his first term, in 1955, he had heavy worries on his mind. After his years as a wartime general, Dwight D. Eisenhower wanted most of all a lasting peace. Through the North Atlantic Treaty Organization (NATO), he had built a shaky balance in Europe between the communist and non-communist countries, but this was the time of the "Cold War," when Russia's posture was hostile and threatening.

In Asia, the Red Chinese wanted to take Formosa, where America's former ally Chiang Kai-Shek was holding out with a small army. At home in America, the "hard liners"—powerful senators in the President's own Republican Party—believed America should go to war to keep Formosa from the Red Chinese. They pressured the President to make belligerent statements and threats.

Peace remained President Eisenhower's top priority. In July, he attended a meeting of the heads of Britain, France, Russia, and the United States in Geneva, Switzerland. He wanted to make progress toward a nuclear disarmament agreement with the Russians. Although his trusted friend, the Secretary of State John Foster Dulles, warned him not to be too hopeful, the President's spirits were high as he prepared to leave for Geneva. As I watched him depart with Mrs. Eisenhower and his son John, I thought about how the hopes of the world rode with this optimistic man.

Early at the conference, President Eisenhower spoke directly to the Russians, especially to his old wartime friend, Marshall Zhukov.

He said, "I would like my friend Marshall Zhukov to listen carefully. . . . I have known him for a long time and he knows that speaking as soldier to soldier, I have never uttered a single word that I did not believe to be the truth."

On the fourth day of the meeting, speaking naturally, without notes, President Eisenhower made his surprising new proposal, which was known as "Open Skies."

He proposed that Russia and America each "give the other a complete blueprint of our military establishment . . . to provide within our country facilities for aerial photography to the other country . . . you can make all the pictures you choose and take them to your country to study. . . ."

The Russians were stunned and silent. They dared not to immediately trample down such a positive idea, and they had no new ideas ready to offer themselves.

From all over the world came messages of support for President Eisenhower's courage. The Geneva Conference was a great personal triumph for him.

But back in Washington, I saw the President's spirits sag. He hadn't brought back any new agreement with the Russians. The day when the big powers would lay down their arms was still far away.

I was glad the First Family was going to Denver in late August. Both the President and Mrs. Eisenhower looked worn out after Geneva. In Denver, the First Lady would visit her mother, Mrs. Doud, and the President would golf, fish, and camp outdoors with friends.

On September 23, Dwight D. Eisenhower, then sixty-four years old, got up at dawn at Byers Peak Ranch to cook his own flapjacks, mush, and sausage. Back in Denver, he worked for two hours in his office, then played eighteen holes of golf before lunch and nine holes afterward. In the middle of the night, the President woke up with severe chest pains. He was having a coronary thrombosis: a heart attack.

I came to work that day to a grim White House. But when Mrs. Eisenhower called J.B. West to reassure everyone that the President was out of danger, we were joyful.

There was a special spirit in the White House while the President was recovering in Denver. It was as if all of us on the staff wanted everything to be perfect at the house, thinking that would somehow help the President get better. We acted like a big family.

At last, on November 11, the President and Mrs. Eisenhower were due to return. The house shone with spit and polish.

President Eisenhower looked tanned and fit as he walked into the White House. I took him to the elevator, then he stopped.

"Wait a minute, Bruce," he said, "the doctors want me to walk up the steps sometimes to strengthen my heart!"

Only six weeks after a coronary, and he was ready to climb stairs. You couldn't keep President Eisenhower down. Many people thought he wouldn't run for reelection after his heart attack, but they were wrong.

The presidential election of 1956 was hard. As the campaign reached its height, the Middle East erupted. Israel and her Arab neighbors were at sword's point. Britain's Prime Minister Anthony Eden had tried to persuade President Eisenhower to join with the English and the French in sending a military "peacekeeping" force to the trouble spot, but the President said no —only the United Nations should do that job, that was what it was created for.

The very week of the final election, in November, Britain, France, and Israel seized the Suez Canal without telling the United States in advance. President Eisenhower was outraged—I had never seen him so upset. That same week the Russians crushed the revolt against them in Hungary. Narrowly, the President managed to keep us out of war in both places, and he was reelected by a big majority. My admiration for him grew.

By 1957 the President and I had become close. He was especially interested in my son, Preston, Jr. Preston had grown up with a passion for sports, above all, baseball. Many were the times I had to go to the diamond and drag him home to his schoolbooks. I took a dim view of his passion for baseball. I saw it as a chancy career with no long-term security. But in high school he had developed a strong right pitching arm and a wicked curve ball.

After graduation Preston, six-feet four, was recruited by the coach from Lyndon Teacher's College, Vermont. He was the first black student at Lyndon, and he made friends, studied science, and earned letters in soccer, basketball, and baseball.

Every spring the Lyndon baseball team traveled to play ball at other colleges. On a visit to Baltimore in the spring of 1957, a lunchroom waitress, backed by the restaurant manager, served every member of the team except Preston, who was the only black. Furious, my son walked out and, to his surprise, every member of his team walked out with him, leaving their food behind.

President Eisenhower invited Preston and his teammates to the Oval Office. Flashbulbs popped as Preston gave the President a large can of Vermont maple syrup for his flapjacks.

In June, the President asked me if Preston was still playing ball, and I said there was no way I could stop his determination to make the Big Leagues.

I must have sounded glum because the President asked me, "What's the matter? Aren't you pleased your son is so talented?"

"To be honest with you, I'm not, Mr. President," I replied. "I say schooling first and baseball second. My son has one more year of college. If he's tapped by the Majors, I'm afraid he won't finish. He's a science major and teaching science would be a great career, but he has to graduate from college to be a teacher."

"But Bruce," the President persisted, "wouldn't you be proud to see him a famous baseball star? Think of the big money he'd make!"

"Suppose he got hurt?" I countered. "Then where would he be, with an unfinished education? To tell the truth, Mr. President, I don't much like baseball and never did. My son dragged me to it by force."

One evening two weeks later when I came home from work, Preston jumped up from his chair to meet me.

"Dad!" he said. "I went to the pro-ball tryouts today at Griffiths Stadium and the scouts there are interested in me! They want me down at Wheeling, West Virginia, on Thursday at nine A.M. Will you take me?"

I didn't have the heart to turn him down, and he promised he'd finish college, regardless.

On Thursday we got up very early and drove to West Virginia. There he was spotted by a scout from the Pittsburgh Pirates and was invited to their training camp in Jacksonville, Florida. Preston was so excited he never stopped talking all the way back to Washington.

At five o'clock that afternoon I met the President coming back from the Oval Office. As he got off the elevator at the second floor I told him that my ballplayer had gotten picked by the Pirates' scouts that day.

I got a mischievous smile from the President. He gloated.

"See Bruce, I told you he has to have his head! Now you'll never believe this, but this very evening my old friend Branch Rickey, president of the Pirates, is coming to my stag dinner. You can be sure I'll tell him about your son."

On the way downstairs I thought to myself, I just wish the President wasn't such an avid sports fan. And why can't I keep quiet.

That evening, I was sitting in the Usher's Office manning one of the phones, while the President and his friends were having dinner. Eugene Allen came rushing in, telling me to get on over to the lobby. The President wanted me. I wondered what could be the matter. The President hadn't yet had time to have cigars and coffee with his guests. It was too early for him to go upstairs.

In the lobby I saw the President with a brown-haired plump man in his early sixties. That's when he introduced me to his friend Branch Rickey.

Mr. Rickey pumped my hand and questioned me closely about Preston. I had to be honest and tell him how well Preston was playing. I finished by stating that I intended for him to finish his schooling, however.

Mr. Rickey took a little notebook from his pocket and wrote down all the details.

"I understand your feeling, Mr. Bruce," he said, "but I intend to follow your son's career. He sounds very promising."

Preston went to training camp and worked hard. Then he went back to college in September. In January he got a letter from the Pirates' talent scout Joe Bowen, ordering him to report to Jacksonville, Florida, for spring training. He told Preston to do a lot of running in the meantime.

Before Preston left for Jacksonville at the start of his spring vacation, he once again promised me he'd report back to college to graduate with his class. But I knew I couldn't *make* my son follow my orders, and those baseball owners had all the money in the world to offer him.

Preston called me long distance from Florida.

"Dad!" he cried, "they want to sign me on!"

"Okay son," I said. "I'll be right down."

In Jacksonville, my son and I met with Branch Rickey and talent scout Mr. Boyd. They were ready to grab Preston, fast.

I said to Mr. Boyd, "If you want him after he gets his education, fine. If not, just call the whole thing off! I'm going to finish *my* job and see that my son gets his schooling."

Mr. Boyd agreed to my terms and the Pirates' contract gave my son a thousand dollar bonus. Mr. Boyd said that when Preston graduated, he would go to the Pirates' Class A farm team in Lincoln, Nebraska.

I felt relieved and ready to forget baseball for a while.

But the next morning, April 13, 1958, at the Jacksonville Airport, I picked up a copy of *The New York Times* to see this headline: PRESIDENT TURNS BASEBALL SCOUT.

The story was about me and my son, Branch Rickey and President Eisenhower. It told about Jim Haggerty's press briefing the day before. Newsmen had nagged Mr. Haggerty, didn't the President know that science teachers were in short supply? Didn't the country need science teachers more than ballplayers? One newsman had asked Mr. Haggerty, why doesn't the President scout for the Washington Senators? This broke up the crowd. The poor Washington Senators were down in the cellar, in eighth place in their league; they could use the President's help.

Next morning newspapers all over the country had picked up the story. That evening, President Eisenhower was having dinner upstairs with his brother Dr. Milton Eisenhower and friends. I went upstairs with the list of movies the projectionist had ready to show.

I dreaded to meet the President, not knowing if the critical tone of the press had upset him.

From the West Hall the President called out to me, "Bruce, come on in here! You know at my news conference today, some of the reporters asked me about Preston. How's he doing?"

I told the President my son was fine.

He said, "Well, I set them straight. By God I am proud of him. I want you to tell him that!"

That summer, while playing ball in Nebraska, Preston was offered a job teaching science, math, and literature in the tiny town of Readsboro, Vermont. The Pirates agreed to his teaching over the winter. Preston gave himself only a day or two to rest in Washington before going to Vermont. I noticed he was very tired. To celebrate his college graduation and his new job, I bought him a new green Plymouth sedan and kept his old Ford for myself.

Preston phoned us from Readsboro to tell us he loved the little town up in the mountains, the school, and the family he lived with, the Ecchers.

Two days later, just as Preston was to turn twenty-one, the phone rang. It was a long distance operator from Vermont. She said, "Mr. Bruce? Mr. Morrissey is on the line."

A chill came over me. Who was Mr. Morrissey?

"Mr. Bruce, I am Andy Morrissey, the superintendent of schools in Readsboro. First, I want to tell you that your son is all right."

My knees trembled.

Mr. Morrissey continued: "He was in an accident. His car went off the road. You should come as soon as you can, but don't worry. He's going to be all right."

The phone rang again. It was Jim Haggerty, who told me, "The President just called from Rhode Island. He learned of your son's accident over the radio. He wants you to get ready to go to Vermont immediately. Let us know if you need anything. We'll be in touch."

He added, "The President has talked to his physician, General Snyder, and General Snyder has already talked to the doctors up there. Your son is still in the operating room, but he's stabilized. He's lost a lot of blood, but they've given him transfusions."

I left for Vermont, not knowing if the old Ford would make it up there or not. At New York the news came on the car radio, and I heard:

"Preston Bruce, Jr., rookie ballplayer for the Pittsburgh Pirates and son of White House Doorman Preston Bruce, has been injured in a car accident in Readsboro, Vermont. The President has made sure everything possible is being done for young Mr. Bruce."

I drove very fast. In Springfield, Massachusetts, a police car, red light flashing and siren blaring, forced me off the road. The officer stuck his head in my window. He had on leggings and he looked tough.

"What's the hurry?" he barked.

"My car is under control," I answered. "I've come up from Washington. My son was in an accident in Vermont."

Like magic the officer's manner changed. He'd heard about Preston on the radio. All he said was that he knew how much I wanted to get there, but I must cut down on my speed.

I made it safely to the hospital at North Adams, Massachusetts. No one asked me to sign any forms or pay anything. I was in a daze. All I could think of was, please, don't let anything happen to my son.

In the hallway, a bright-eyed little man with foxy red hair came up to me and said, "Mr. Bruce, I'm your son's doctor. My name is H. Y. Twist. He's doing very well, after all he's been through. I've been in touch with Dr. Snyder in Washington, and President Eisenhower has ordered specialists if necessary—anything we want—the sky's the limit. They must think the world of you and your son."

I felt Preston must be in terrible shape to need all this attention.

Dr. Twist told me, "Your son fell asleep at the wheel on Mohawk Mountain, and the car went over the side. Thirty feet down it was held by three small trees. His face took the brunt of the accident. It took him four hours to crawl up the steep ravine, bleeding heavily. Partway up he blacked out and would have bled to death, but it started to rain and that revived him. At the nearest house, there was a big husky guard dog on the porch. That dog just stood by and watched as your son hauled himself up the steps and collapsed at the doorway. The lady there—Mrs. Viola Guetti—wrapped Preston in blankets and called the ambulance. It was a miracle, what your son did. He saved his own life."

I asked Dr. Twist about Preston's face and his eyes.

The doctor said, "Mr. Bruce, I'm a plastic surgeon with twenty years' experience. I'm going to make your son almost as good as new. One eye is okay, but he may lose the sight in the other. He's young and healthy, and he's going to make an excellent recovery."

As Dr. Twist guided me down the corridor, he told me that President Eisenhower had ordered Preston moved to a private room. Inside that room, crowded with flowers, cards, and gifts from the people at Readsboro, I saw nurses bending over Preston, who seemed completely enveloped in bandages. Then he stuck his big head up, his eyes totally covered, and he spoke.

"I hear my Daddy walking."

Preston couldn't see anything but he knew my walk.

The nurses cried, I cried, and inside his bandages, Preston cried.

He reached his arm up, and I grabbed it.

"Daddy," said Preston. "Dr. Twist took over two hundred stitches in my face and sewed my nose back together. He's the greatest!"

Superintendent Morrissey came in and told me that Preston's class would be taught by a priest from the village and that he would draw his salary while he was recovering. He said that Silvio and Minna Eccher and their son Stephen, with whom Preston lived, were broken up by Preston's accident and insisted that I stay with them.

The day I left for Washington, Dr. Twist removed the bandages from one of Preston's eyes so he could see again. A few weeks later, when more bandages were removed, Preston found he could see out of the other eye too.

When he came out of the hospital, the Ecchers took care of him while his wounds healed and his strength came back. Our two families have been close ever since that time.

After Christmas vacation with us in Washington, he went back to teach school at Readsboro. He found a way to repay the kindnesses shown him by the townspeople. The Readsboro school was cramped and small. Teachers and parents wanted a new one, but so far the citizens had not voted the money needed for a new school.

Preston campaigned for the new school. Freshly bandaged from continuing plastic surgery, he traveled the countryside to argue for a new school with a large all-purpose room for young and old to use for meetings, plays, and evening classes. He helped to make the case.

The needed $300,000 was voted, and the school was built.

Two years later, when John F. Kennedy was President, Dwight D. Eisenhower came to the White House for lunch, and I had some news for him. My son had a new job. He was principal of Readsboro School, the first black to be a school principal in the history of the state of Vermont.

Mr. Eisenhower was very pleased, then he asked me, "Does Preston still play ball?"

"Not much," I answered, "that car accident spoiled his pitching arm and he's subject to blackouts."

"Does he miss it a lot?" he asked.

"Of course," I replied. "Baseball was always his first love. He'll always miss it. But he told me that when a child's face suddenly lights up with understanding while he's explaining a point, it's as exciting for him as any moment he ever knew in sports."

Mr. Eisenhower admitted I'd been right to insist on Preston's diploma. I thanked him and I said, "I'm glad my son got his chance at baseball. But my father struggled so hard to keep me in school, I had to do the same for Preston."

When President Eisenhower personally intervened to help Preston after his accident in Vermont, it meant all the more to me because at that exact time, September 1958, the President was struggling to hold onto his most valued aide, Governor Sherman Adams.

The mid-term congressional elections of 1958 loomed, and all the polls showed the Republicans in deep trouble. In past elections, Richard Nixon had been the Republican Party's toughest spokesman, but this time he stayed aloof, preferring to make friends rather than enemies, as he prepared for his own race for President in 1960.

So, in Nixon's place, the President sent Governor Adams out around the country to attack the Democrats.

No one had voted to elect Sherman Adams—he was an appointed official—and he had angered many people during his years of great power as the President's right-hand man. Then he made the mistake of taking some expensive presents from his old friend, businessman Bernard Goldfine, who was under scrutiny for possible wrong-doing by two government agencies. That gave Adams's enemies the perfect weapon. Powerful Democrats in the Congress, aided by hard-line conservative Republicans, raised an outcry in the press. The President had to give in and let Governor Adams go.

The mid-term elections gave the Democrats a landslide victory, so the President lost his majority in Congress. And within days of the election, Soviet Premier Nikita Khrushchev in Moscow threatened to provoke a major crisis between Russia and the United States over the divided city of Berlin.

While the President was coping with all these reverses, his close friend and trusted Secretary of State, John Foster Dulles, was desperately ill and died the following April.

By this time, many people expected the last year and a half of the Eisenhower presidency to be a downhill slide. But they didn't know Dwight D. Eisenhower.

With renewed courage and optimism, he decided on a bold gamble. He would invite Premier Khrushchev to visit the United States.

This state visit, which began on September 15, 1959, was unlike any other during my years at the White House.

Born in a hut of mud and reeds, a boy shepherd and child coal miner, Khrushchev was in his twenties when he first learned to read and write. Tough and brilliant, he rose quickly to the very top of the Communist Party. Now, at the pinnacle of power, he was hungry to come to America. He would be the first Russian head of state in history to walk in the front door of the White House as the President's guest. That would show the world that Russia was equal in power to the United States.

President Eisenhower elected to give Khrushchev that satisfaction. But in return he'd sieze the chance to pin him down on such hard questions as a nuclear-test-ban treaty and divided Berlin. In place of the usual hostile insults hurled between Moscow and Washington, President Eisenhower opened the door to his home. To show more good faith, he ordered that all nuclear bomb testing be stopped for the rest of the year. Thus he signaled a new "thaw" in the cold war.

The President's invitation to Mr. Khrushchev was greeted with alarm. Would the American President submit to Russia's demands? Would the very invitation seem to show approval of Khrushchev? These were the fears at home and abroad.

On August 26, three weeks before the planned state visit by Khrushchev, President Eisenhower left the White House for Europe to calm those fears. In Ger-

many, England, and France, he got an astonishing welcome, an outpouring of love stored up since World War
II. In a telecast from London with Prime Minister Harold MacMillan, Ike said:

"The people, in the long run, are going to do more
to promote peace than our governments. . . . I think
people want peace so much that one of these days governments had better get out of their way and let them
have it."

The President promised in each country that he'd
give away nothing to Khrushchev, but only try to look
for some common ground.

While the President was abroad, we prepared the
White House and made plans, just as we would have for
any state visit. But tensions mounted. D.C. police expected the worst security problems ever; all leaves
were canceled. Ninety Russians were to come with the
Premier: retainers, advisers, journalists, bureaucrats,
his wife, daughters, and sons-in-law.

Congressmen and senators refused to invite Chairman Khrushchev to speak to them on Capitol Hill, and
a retired army captain sued in court to block the Premier's visit, calling him a "criminal alien." A black
Cadillac toured the city carrying a banner—THE
BUTCHER OF BUDAPEST—referring to the crushed
Hungarian revolt. In the back seat sat a man resem-
bling Khrushchev carrying spades, to remind people of
Khrushchev's taunt to the United States: "We will bury
you."

When the President returned from Europe he went
on TV to soothe the American people. He explained, "I
want him to see what America and Americans are like

—to see and feel a great nation living in real freedom." He went on to prod Khrushchev to offer new ideas for peace. Then he'd earn world leadership, the President said. And he urged Americans to be polite to the Soviet leader while warning him not to mistake good manners for weakness.

Two days before Khrushchev's arrival, on September 13, I opened my *Washington Post* to read: RUSSIA HITS THE MOON WITH LUNIK II. Exactly timed for the state visit, the Soviets sent an 860-pound missile, carrying a Soviet coat of arms and instruments, to the moon. It was a propaganda field day for Mr. Khrushchev.

The night before Khrushchev's arrival, a big protest rally was held on the Mall. Fifteen thousand black armbands were sold to mourn the Russian-conquered peoples of Hungary, Yugoslavia, Bulgaria, Latvia, and Lithuania. Skull and crossbones flags were handed out. That same evening, churches all over Washington held special prayer services.

In the midst of all this, nothing seemed to rattle the President. On the morning of Thursday, September 15, I took him from the second floor to his waiting bubbletop limousine. He stood silent in the elevator, deep in thought, dressed in a dark suit, gray silk tie, and white shirt, holding his soft, gray fedora. He was on his way to Andrews Air Force Base to collect his Russian guests. As I stood on the White House steps to watch him go, I could see the protestors gathering in Lafayette Square.

In the Usher's Office we crowded around the TV set. On the runway at Andrews we saw the President and other dignitaries waiting impatiently for the Russian TU-114 turbo-prop. This remarkable plane was so huge that a special stairway of twenty-seven steps had been built for it and mounted on a two and a half ton U.S. Air Force truck. At last, twenty minutes late, the plane landed and down the steps came short, square Nikita Khrushchev to meet our President.

While the Khrushchevs had lunch at Blair House, President Eisenhower came back to the White House. Then, at exactly 2:55 P.M. I brought him down to the North Door. We stood outside together in the humid September sunshine. With us were the new Secretary of State, Christian Herter, United Nations Ambassador Henry Cabot Lodge, and other officials. The President frowned and looked at his watch. His mouth tightened. Already that morning he had waited far too long in the hot sun for the jet full of Russians.

At 3:03 P.M. I saw a limousine enter the circular driveway and drive slowly toward us. A stiff young military aide stood ready to open the car door.

First out was Chairman Khrushchev himself, followed by several aides. Up the steps he hurried, holding a small model of Lunik II. His gait was awkward, a sort of waddle.

During the official greetings and introductions, I studied Nikita Khrushchev. I was not impressed. His head was over-large for his squat frame, completely bald, with small ears set close. Khrushchev's face was coarse—his lower lip hung open showing black crooked teeth and his jaw was thrust forward, defiantly. Under thick black eyebrows, which met over his large nose, his small sharp eyes darted intently this way and that. He had a receding chin and a thick bulldog neck with heavy jowls.

Chairman Khrushchev wore a natty suit of dark silk

and a pearl white silk tie with a thin center line of light blue. His custom-made white shirt had French cuffs with solid gold cuff links. On his feet were hand-made Italian shoes. But his stylish clothes did not suit him, and could not cover up his rough looks and manner.

At the end of the formalities, the President's face suddenly took on a lively expression. Abruptly he pivoted toward me and took my arm. He ordered his interpreter: "I want you to tell Chairman Khrushchev that this is Preston Bruce, an important member of our White House family."

The President shoved me forward to meet the Soviet Premier. From the corner of his mouth, he commanded me: "Shake hands, Bruce."

I put out my hand.

Mr. Khrushchev's head jerked as if someone behind him had pulled a string. He was startled, knocked off base. You could tell that never in his life had he wanted or expected to shake hands with a black man.

I said, "I'm glad to meet you, your Excellency."

Mr. Khrushchev grunted in response.

I saw astonished expressions on the faces of the other Russian officials.

After talking together in the Oval Office, the President and Premier Khrushchev came back to the main hallway. I brought them to the South Entrance, and as I opened the big door, the loud rattle of a jungle green Marine helicopter engine filled the White House. I watched the President take his guest on board and open up a map of Washington, which he put on Mr. Khrushchev's lap.

While the Soviet leader saw the sights of Washington

from the sky, hectic preparations got underway for the state dinner that evening. It was to be the largest ever —one hundred guests from all over the United States.

At 5:30 P.M. the Russians went back to Blair House to rest before dinner, and at 6:00 P.M. I brought down Mrs. Eisenhower as usual to look over the State Dining Room. She was preoccupied, not in her usual gay way before a party.

At 6:55 J. B. West told me, "All right, Bruce, you can go upstairs and bring down the President and Mrs. Eisenhower. The Russians have just left Blair House. This time the President won't have to wait."

On the second floor, the President, dressed in white tie and tails, was pacing back and forth in the West Hall. He barked to Colonel Schultz, "Where in the devil is Mrs. Eisenhower?"

The First Lady popped out of her bedroom dressed in her finest gold brocade ball gown with a full skirt and train. She wore long white kid gloves, diamond earrings, and a diamond and pearl necklace.

Downstairs in the Lobby, President and Mrs. Eisenhower moved toward the arriving Russians as I followed behind. Every one of the Russian men, led by Premier Khrushchev, wore a sober dark business suit. Even Soviet Ambassador Menshikov, who normally showed up at the White House in a splendid top hat and full evening dress, had on a plain business suit.

Chairman and Mrs. Khrushchev carried gifts for President and Mrs. Eisenhower—a shotgun, a jewel box, bottles of vodka and wine, an album of phonograph records, an elk's head, and twelve jars of caviar.

Then it was time for the President and First Lady to

take their guests upstairs to the Yellow Oval Room for a small reception, while all the other guests were arriving downstairs. I had a list of just exactly who was supposed to go upstairs—about eight Russian officials and eight Americans.

As this official party began to climb the Grand Staircase, there was a surge of moving bodies. The other Russian men, chests out, elbows chopping, pushing, and shoving, tried to follow their leader up the stairs.

The Secret Service instantly went into action. They called their buddies for help, and the military aides pitched in too. They confined everyone who wasn't invited upstairs to the first floor.

At 8:00 P.M., when the Marine Band struck up "Ruffles and Flourishes," I watched the two world leaders come back down the Grand Staircase.

Khrushchev fairly seemed to strut his way down the steps while the President, with a hint of a smile on his smooth face, stepped down briskly in time to the music. Behind the two men came their two wives. Mrs. Eisenhower smiled reassuringly at Mrs. Khrushchev, who seemed ill at ease in her dark blue dinner dress with its high neck and elbow-length sleeves. She seemed a good-natured, kindly person who never asked for anything. Throughout the visit, whenever I guided her to the elevator, she smiled and thanked me, unlike her husband.

Mrs. Eisenhower chose to give her Russian guests an all-American menu: roast turkey with cornbread stuffing, Boston brown bread, cranberry sauce, sweet potatoes with pineapple, green beans, lime ice, and ladyfingers.

When it was time for the toasts, I looked at President Eisenhower and Premier Khrushchev sitting side by side. The hopes of the world were pinned on those two people. I remembered something Nikita Khrushchev had once said:

"International tension is like a cabbage. If you tear off the leaves one by one you come to the heart—and the heart of the matter is relations between America and the Soviet Union."

The President rose to his feet, turned toward his Russian guest, raised his glass and said, in part:

"Skillful debate is not now enough. We must depend upon fact and truth. . . . Because of our strength in the world it is vital that we understand each other."

Premier Khrushchev replied:

"Our countries are much too strong. We cannot quarrel with each other. . . . Our countries have different social systems—we believe ours to be better, you believe yours to be better. But we should not bring quarrels to open struggle. Let history judge which of us is right. A good beginning has been made."

The rest of the evening passed quickly. Fred Waring played a program of best-loved American songs ending up with a rousing "Battle Hymn of the Republic." The Russians were swept off to Blair House, leaving all of us at the White House to sigh in relief that the big day had ended without mishap.

Next Mr. Khrushchev toured America, through the farm belt, out to California, and back to Washington. The more Americans he met, the more he mellowed. At the end of his trip, touring a factory in Pittsburgh, Pennsylvania, he admitted, "I don't say that all you have is bad and all we have is good. We can learn from you."

Chairman Khrushchev came back to Washington for more talks with President Eisenhower at Camp David. The two leaders agreed to meet again at a summit conference within a few months. As Nikita Khrushchev left for Moscow he cried, "Thank you, as we say in Russia, for your bread and salt."

For President Eisenhower the Khrushchev state visit was only one of his many efforts toward peace, but for me, it was a highlight of my years at the White House. I was proud of the President for bringing it off, and proud that I was there when it happened. Before and during the Russian visit, President Eisenhower showed his best qualities: his hope, his dignified courtesy, his strong and careful leadership.

The Eisenhowers' last year at the White House sped by. On May 10, 1960, I brought the First Lady some great news—the birth of my first grandchild. Mrs. Eisenhower sent my daughter Elaine two dozen Mamie Eisenhower carnations (which disappeared overnight as mementos for the nurses), and she sent a card to the baby, saying, "Welcome, William Bruce Pryor, to this wonderful world." In her notebook she put down the date of Billy's birth.

I was terribly sad to see the Eisenhowers go when his term was over. They were everything I felt a President and First Lady should be—disciplined and efficient, dignified, serious, and fair. Yet they enjoyed themselves. They were generous, they were friendly, and they were so human, with their funny foibles and their fondness for each other.

When President Eisenhower carried on important conversations in my hearing with top officials, he let me know that he trusted me. For the past seven years, I'd learned the ropes at the White House under the Eisenhowers, and I didn't see how I could ever feel the same way about another First Family. But I knew they deserved to rest and relax in Gettysburg.

Ten years later, in August 1970, after President Eisenhower's death in 1969, Mrs. Eisenhower checked her notebook and saw that my grandson, Billy Pryor, was then ten years old. She invited three generations of our family—me, my son Preston, Jr., and Billy—to visit her at Gettysburg.

It was a great day. Mrs. Eisenhower showed us all over the farm, then she took Billy into the study and turned him loose with General Eisenhower's pile of scrapbooks. Later, we sat on the porch and discussed our two families. Every year thereafter until her death, I called on Mamie Eisenhower at Gettysburg and we would reminisce together.

I look back on my years with the Eisenhowers as the happiest of my time at the White House.

# Chapter 3

# THE KENNEDYS

AT 11:00 A.M. on January 21, 1961, Inauguration Day, I stood by the North Door of the White House. In the lobby nearby were mounds of packing boxes and luggage. In less than three hours, President and Mrs. Eisenhower would leave the White House. Earlier that morning, I'd stood in line with all eighty of my colleagues on the household staff for the traditional goodbye ceremony—the first in my experience. I hoped there'd be time for me to have a private moment with the President and First Lady.

Every few minutes, I went outside into the bitter cold to scan the newly cleared driveway. I squinted from the glare of the bright sunshine on the fresh snow that covered the White House grounds. I was watching for young John Fitzgerald Kennedy, who today would replace Dwight D. Eisenhower as President of the United States. Soon, without stopping at the sentry gate, a black limousine came up the driveway, its big tires crunching on the snow.

Two young people brushed past me with polite nods. I got only a quick impression of a debonair young man, who yanked off his top hat as he reached the top of the steps, showing a shock of thick reddish-brown hair. With him was his beautiful wife. She was even younger, and had large dark eyes and dark hair. She was dressed in a simple bright-colored wool coat, a small fur hat perched on the back of her head.

In the lobby, President and Mrs. Eisenhower greeted the Kennedys warmly, and took them to the Red Room for coffee. Republican President Eisenhower had told me he believed Democrat John F. Kennedy to be the better of the two candidates in the recent hard-fought election. President Eisenhower had made only one campaign speech for the Republican candidate, Vice-President Richard M. Nixon.

Coffee over, I stood in the lobby holding the President's swallow-tailed black morning coat and top hat. As he came out of the Red Room, Dwight Eisenhower saw me, and said, "Well, Bruce. Thank you for your help these past seven years. Mrs. Eisenhower and I will miss you, but we don't intend to lose track of you."

He then turned to Senator Kennedy and said, "This is Preston Bruce. He will be one of the most loyal, trusted members of your staff. He's a true gentleman and you can depend upon him."

Senator Kennedy and I shook hands, and he told me, "Those are high marks. I expect we'll have good times together, Mr. Bruce."

At this, our first meeting, I felt that John Kennedy saw me as the old man of the mountain.

President and Mrs. Eisenhower and Senator and Mrs. Kennedy left for the U.S. Capitol. There on the plaza, in the freezing wind, bundled in sleeping bags and blankets, a great crowd waited to see the awesome power of the American presidency pass from one man to another.

High up on the porch of the Capitol, the elderly poet Robert Frost spoke for John Kennedy. Never before in United States history had a poet been asked to take part in an inauguration.

With John Kennedy at his side, Robert Frost began to read his new poem:

> "Summoning artists to participate
> In the august occasions of the state
> Seems something artists ought to celebrate."

At nine minutes to one o'clock, the Chief Justice stood ready to administer the Oath of Office to Senator Kennedy. This was the heart of the inauguration. At the White House we stood silent, listening to the radio. John Fitzgerald Kennedy raised his right hand and put his left hand on the Fitzgerald family Bible. His voice rang out in the sharp clear air:

"I do solemnly swear that I will faithfully execute the Office of President of the United States, and will to the best of my ability, preserve, protect, and defend the Constitution of the United States."

Now President Kennedy gave his inaugural address. I was gripped by his call to action, his faith in the power of young leadership. He said:

"Let the word go forth . . . that the torch has been passed to a new generation. . . . Let every nation know, whether it wishes us well or ill, that we shall pay any price, bear any burden, meet any hardship, support any friend, oppose any foe, in order to assure the survival and the success of liberty. . . . And so, my fellow Americans: Ask not what your country can do for you—ask what you can do for your country. . . . My fellow citizens of the world: Ask not what America will do for you but what together we can do for the freedom of mankind."

The new President and Mrs. Kennedy left Capitol Hill for the reviewing stand in front of the White House where they'd watch the inaugural parade. I hurried down to Pennsylvania Avenue with warm blankets from the White House. Mrs. Kennedy let me wrap her up against the cold, but the President wouldn't use a blanket. He stood up to review the marching bands and crack military units that passed by. I heard him say to an aide, "Look at that Coast Guard unit! There's not a single black man in it! Why?"

The aide told him, "Mr. President, the Coast Guard Academy doesn't admit blacks."

The President demanded that a report on the Coast Guard be on his desk by morning.

After the parade there was a small reception for the family and a few close friends at the White House. Then the President and First Lady took a short rest before the inaugural balls that evening.

When I went upstairs at 8:00 P.M., President Kennedy introduced me to his wife Jacqueline, who looked stunning in a long white chiffon gown. That dress is now on display at the Smithsonian Institution in Washington along with the inaugural ball gowns of all the other First Ladies.

I then met the President's brother, Robert Kennedy, who was the new Attorney General. I knew that this man's job gave him more power to help black people than any other in Washington, save for that of the President. I knew that during the presidential campaign the two Kennedy brothers had taken a strong stand on racial issues. When Martin Luther King, Jr. was jailed for leading a peaceful protest march in Georgia, frantic Democratic politicians had begged John Kennedy not to show any sympathy. They thought doing so would cost him so many votes he would lose the election. But Senator Kennedy had phoned Mrs. King to express his outrage at her husband's arrest, and Robert Kennedy had phoned the judge who had jailed Dr. King to protest the unjust denial of bail.

The news stories about the Kennedy protests were so embarrassing, the judge had backtracked. He set bail and let Martin Luther King, Jr. go free. Today, many people think that black votes pulled John F. Kennedy through to victory in the close election of 1960.

That evening, Robert Kennedy looked rumpled in his formal evening wear. I soon learned that's the way he always looked. His hair was tousled, and he seemed uncomfortable, as if his elegant clothes were too tight. While his handsome brother put his head back and roared at someone's joke, Bobby Kennedy's expression was serious, his head bowed and shoulders hunched forward as if he were getting ready to sprint. When we met, his ice-blue eyes bore through me. He had no small talk but he reached out for my hand and gripped it.

President and Mrs. Kennedy stayed late at the inaugural balls, then they visited a friend in Georgetown. We waited and waited for them. At two o'clock in the morning, they returned to the White House with friends to celebrate further on the second floor. It was clear that they didn't realize that the household staff had been at work since early morning, and couldn't leave until the President and First Lady were settled down for the night.

At 3:15 A.M. I took the last guest out the North Door and returned upstairs to secure the house. Everyone else had gone home except the Secret Service night shift. It was my job to see if the new President and First Lady needed anything more before they went to sleep.

On the second floor I first went into the West Hall and turned off the lights. As I got to the bedrooms of the President and First Lady, to my surprise the doors were wide open and the rooms empty. I then heard voices from way down at the other end of the White House—the East Hall.

I went down the long corridor and the President's voice called out, "Is that you, Bruce? I'm here in the Lincoln Bedroom."

The Lincoln Bedroom! I couldn't believe it. Every President since Lincoln's day had refused to sleep in that room—they'd all feared the room would bring them misfortune. Now, here was our young President relaxing in President Lincoln's big black four-poster bed with its, ornately carved headboard, as if it were the most natural place in the world for him to be.

"Can you open the window, Bruce?" said the President.

The White House windows are enormous, and the President had to be careful of his back because of an injury during World War II. I tugged and strained. The over-sized window hadn't been opened in years, if ever. At last I got it open and a blast of zero degree air poured into the bedroom. The President sighed with pleasure.

Then he said, "I'd like a Coke, please, Bruce."

From across the hall in the Queen's Bedroom, Mrs. Kennedy's little voice chimed in, "And please get me a Dubonnet over ice."

After hunting around downstairs in the empty pantries, I found the drinks, filled two glasses with ice and carried it all upstairs. The President took his glass, dumped the ice out on the tray, and gulped down the warm Coke.

"Thanks, Bruce, and good night," he said, with a big smile. When John Kennedy smiled, you couldn't help but smile with him.

I got home at 4:00 A.M., completely exhausted. It was going to be a struggle to keep up with the Kennedys.

When I got to work the next afternoon, the Usher's Office was in an uproar. Everyone was upset. Usher Tom Carter summed it up:

"Neither the President nor the First Lady know the meaning of the word security. They don't tell us their plans, and they have no regular habits."

When I took the President and Mrs. Kennedy upstairs after dinner that night, I was certain they would be so tired after the festivities of inauguration day that we could all relax.

But I was wrong.

Bang! The elevator door opened in the hallway across from the Usher's Office. Out popped the President. He charged down the hall, the Secret Service in hot pursuit. Where could he be going at this hour?

The President slammed straight out the Northwest Door and took off into the frigid winter night. He wore no coat, no hat, and no galoshes for the snow. Only twenty-four hours in the White House, and he had to escape. Once outside, he went straight out the North Gate to Pennsylvania Avenue, and strolled off into the night as if he were just any young man.

But he wasn't just any young man. The Secret Service couldn't allow him to do that again. He would take his walks within the White House grounds. He had eighteen acres to hike around in, but he wanted to get outside that fence.

The Secret Service took away the President's freedom, and I made him wear an overcoat and rubbers. I wasn't about to sit back and let him catch pneumonia.

The President's valet, George Thomas, and I soon became friends. George gave me two pairs of rubbers and two overcoats: one set for the first floor and one for the ground floor. That way, I could nab the President at whichever door he chose to depart from.

"Mr. President, just put these on," I'd say, holding up his galoshes. He would give me a funny look and lift up his foot for me to slip the hated things on. Sometimes he just *wouldn't* put them on. He was like a little schoolboy, bound to run off unprotected into the cold. It was pretty clear that he knew I was enjoying the game with him.

The next problem was where to meet the President after he finished his walk? I could only be at one entrance at a time. A President is *never* allowed to stand around outside a White House door. I should be there waiting for him. The Secret Service men didn't have walkie-talkies then. One of them would run to find a phone and call in to tell us which way the President was heading back into the White House. President Kennedy knew he was causing us problems, but for a long time it never dawned on him that he ought to do something about it.

Bedtime for the new President and First Lady was another headache.

The Eisenhowers had stuck to a schedule that could be depended on. Every night at ten o'clock when I'd go up to secure the house, they'd be settled into bed for the night, their bedroom doors safely closed.

But the Kennedys were night owls, and I never knew what to expect. Several times as I came down the East Hall I interrupted the President and Mrs. Kennedy, in skimpy nightclothes, scampering back and forth across the hall to each other's bedrooms. I was embarrassed even though they didn't seem to mind.

During a quiet moment in the Usher's Office, I consulted J. B. West. "I've got this sticky situation on the second floor in the evenings. I know I must secure the house, but I never know what I'll run into when I go up there. The President and Mrs. Kennedy are a young couple, and I don't like to intrude on their privacy."

J. B. looked startled. He said nothing. I asked him point-blank, "Will you ask them when I should come upstairs to secure the floor?"

J.B. looked off into space. He didn't want to deal with

this any more than I did. Then the phone rang in the Usher's Office and he put his attention to a problem more easily solved than the one I'd posed.

As the days went by I felt more and more frustrated and worried. Finally I made up my mind. If the Chief Usher wouldn't ask the President and First Lady about this, I would have to.

One evening, the President and Mrs. Kennedy came back to the White House after a dinner party. I met them at the East Entrance. As they came through the Diplomatic Reception Room they were very lovey-dovey, kissing and hugging each other.

I took them upstairs in the elevator, thinking that now is the time to talk to them. I was having trouble getting up my nerve. On the second floor, the Kennedys smiled and said, "Good night, Bruce," the way they always did. They then started to go off down the hall.

But instead of wishing them good night, I said, "President and Mrs. Kennedy, may I ask you a question?"

They stopped, turned around, and came back to where I was standing next to the elevator.

"Certainly, Bruce," said the President, "What is it?"

I said, "Perhaps I shouldn't ask you this, but I'd be very happy if you'd tell me how I should secure the lights in your section of the house."

The President asked, "Well, how did you do it before?"

I answered, "We turned the lights out at ten o'clock each night in all the rooms that can be seen from the outside of the house."

He said, "Well, you do it just the way you've always done it."

That wasn't the answer I needed.

I continued, "When it comes to your area, should I come in there to put them out?"

"Yes, sure, come right ahead," the President said in a casual tone.

All the time Mrs. Kennedy was listening. She had a twinkle in her eye. Finally she spoke up.

"Don't worry, Bruce," she said. "We know you're married too,"

Mrs. Kennedy settled the matter. From then on I went upstairs at ten o'clock to secure the house on schedule. And from that night on, I knew that Mrs. Kennedy could be depended on to come up with the answers to problems.

Mrs. Kennedy's good judgment showed in her choice of Social Secretary. Tall, blond, beautiful, and brainy, Letitia Baldridge won our hearts from the day she arrived. Her attitude was, please show me how things should be done at the White House. She came to us for advice, and was grateful when we gave it.

Miss Baldridge and J. B. West gave me the responsibility to straighten out the mess with the escort cards at state dinners. I had the White House carpenter, Bonner Arrington, construct a special table according to my design. It was high, so I could easily read the names, and it was big enough to hold all the cards. It became known as "Bruce's table." I'd stand behind my table handing out the cards to each dinner guest. Once the system got underway neither the ushers, nor the social aides, nor the military aides touched those cards. There were no more mix-ups.

Six days after the inauguration, Mrs. Kennedy started to tear apart the White House. Her plan was to redeco-

*Preston Bruce's parents, Rancy and Amanda Bruce, as they looked when they were first married.*

*Preston and Virginia Bruce, 1930, at their home in Washington, D.C.*

*Preston Jr. on his first birthday with his father.*

*Elaine Bruce, six months old, with her mother.*

*Virginia and Preston Bruce in front of the White House Christmas tree.*

*An official portrait of Dwight D. Eisenhower, President of the United States, 1953-1961.*

*Preston Bruce, Jr. and his college classmates meet President Eisenhower, as his father looks on.*

*The Eisenhower family at Christmas 1955. Left to right are David, John, Mamie, the President holding Susan, Barbara Jean, and Barbara Ann.*

*President Eisenhower greets Sir Anthony Eden on his January 30, 1956 visit to the White House.*

*Preston Bruce, Preston Jr., and Billy Bruce at Gettysburg with Mamie Eisenhower.*

*An official portrait of John F. Kennedy, President of the United States, 1961–1963.*

*Inaugural Day 1961. President Kennedy leaves the White House accompanied by former President Eisenhower.*

*Jacqueline Kennedy with young Caroline and John Jr.*

*The First Family, Easter 1963, Palm Beach, Florida.*

*The President and John-John at work in the Oval Office.*

*Attorney General Robert Kennedy and Ethel Kennedy and their nine children.*

*The body of John F. Kennedy lies in repose November 23, 1963, in the historic East Room of the White House. The honor guard is comprised of four enlisted men of the Army, Navy, Marines, and Air Force.*

*The body of President Kennedy is borne from the White House.*

*Official photograph of Lyndon B. Johnson, President of the United States, 1963–1969.*

*President Johnson with Blanco and Him.*

*President and Lady Bird Johnson at home at the White House.*

*Lucy Johnson and Patrick Nugent on their wedding day.*

*Official photograph of Richard M. Nixon, President of the United States, 1969–1974.*

*President Richard M. Nixon and Patricia Nixon.*

*Pat Nixon with Virginia and Preston Bruce.*

*An arrival ceremony at the White House south entrance, during the Nixon administration. The policemen's uniforms are new and the subject of considerable controversy.*

*Preston Bruce greets Mrs. Hubert Humphrey, Mrs. Mike Mansfield, and other Senate wives at an afternoon reception during the Nixon administration.*

*President Nixon returning to the White House from a speaking engagement in downtown Washington, D.C.*

*Official photograph of Gerald R. Ford, President of the United States, 1974–1977.*

*President Gerald Ford and Betty Ford and their children.*

*Preston Bruce presents his grandchildren, Stephen, Kellene, Preston III, and Billy, to President Ford.*

*Steve and Susan Ford at Camp David with President and Mrs. Ford.*

*Gerald Ford and Liberty in the Oval Office.*

*Preston Bruce, John Johnson, and Eugene Allen with Sammy Davis, Jr. when he visited the White House in May 1973.*

*The White House.*

*Naval officers, serving as social aides under President Nixon, and Preston Bruce planning for a State Dinner.*

*Secretary of the Treasury David Kennedy is assisted by Mr. Bruce as he arrives at the White House for a State Dinner.*

*February 5, 1975. Preston Bruce is photographed with White House social aides to commemorate his retirement.*

rate from top to bottom, and to redo the second floor to include a family kitchen and dining room. That was why she and her husband had moved into the East Hall.

I was horrified and so was the rest of the staff. We loved the White House as it was and saw no need to change it.

Mrs. Kennedy put on her blue jeans and went to work. She hunted through dusty, cavernous storerooms for antique furniture that had played a part in White House history. She found broken-down old pieces that looked like nothing, and had them mended and restored.

When the Kennedys arrived there was fifty thousand dollars left in the White House budget for repairs that year. Mrs. Kennedy used that up fast, putting in the new dining room and kitchen. There was no money left to buy the furniture she wanted: pieces that had actually been in the White House long ago, or other beautiful old pieces that would fit in well.

So Mrs. Kennedy asked for donations of antique furniture for the White House. She consulted Henry duPont, whose museum of American antiques, Winterthur, outside Wilmington, Delaware, is world famous. Once a month, eighty-year-old Mr. duPont drove down from Wilmington. Mrs. Kennedy took him all over the White House to show him the changes she'd made. She'd show him a picture she'd borrowed from the National Gallery, and look up at him with her big brown eyes and say, "Is this the right place for it, Henry?" There was always someone standing by to move the picture to the exact spot Mr. duPont thought it should go. After the tour, Mrs. Kennedy gave her

guest a delicious lunch cooked by her French chef, Rene Verdon. She told Mr. duPont about the furniture she needed. Mr. duPont always knew how to get it for her.

As Mr. duPont's limousine disappeared down the driveway, Mrs. Kennedy was busy moving everything back the way she had it before. When Mr. duPont came back the next month, he never showed that he noticed that pictures and furniture weren't where he had placed them. He just seemed obviously tickled to be back at the White House having lunch again with Mrs. Kennedy.

Mrs. Kennedy also called in a French decorator, Mr. Budon, and Bill Walton and other members of the Fine Arts Commission for advice. Larry Arata, whom the Kennedys had known for years, came from Hyannisport to upholster and restore the antique furniture.

Mrs. Kennedy often asked the President for his opinion too. She liked to please him. But she always kept the final decision for herself. Her taste was flawless, and when she was finished with the White House, it looked better than it ever had—a living museum of U.S. history for the American people.

A month after the inauguration, I welcomed to the White House two more Kennedys—three-year-old Caroline and baby John-John, two-and-a-half-months-old. They came with their English nanny, Maude Shaw, and their Secret Service men, who were known as the "diaper detail."

I liked big Bob Foster, who protected John-John, and Lynn Meredith, a fatherly man who watched out for Caroline. I was the link between these men and their

charges upstairs. They received the children from me when I brought them downstairs.

The Kennedys enjoyed their children. The minute the President got off the elevator when he went upstairs for his lunch, he'd clap his hands and Caroline would come running, and John-John, too, when he grew big enough. They'd hug him around the knees; then he'd sit on the floor and take them into his lap.

One day I watched the President crawling around on the floor with his squealing children. He got excited and *crack!*—he ran into a glass-topped table, and blood dripped down his face from an ugly gash. Quickly I called the doctor, who patched him up. When the President came downstairs after his lunch and nap, everyone saw the big bandage and teased me that Mrs. Kennedy must have crowned her husband with a lamp.

John-John liked to play under his father's desk in the Oval Office. Sometimes I'd be asked to fetch him because there was business to be done that would be better accomplished without John-John. I'd have to pull him away from his daddy.

Jacqueline Kennedy was like a mother bear with her cubs where her children were concerned. She set aside a chunk of time every afternoon for her children, and *nothing* was allowed to interfere. If the Social Office scheduled something for her at that time, she wouldn't go—someone had to fill in for her. Mrs. Kennedy was a loner. She fought for her privacy. She didn't want anyone around her when she had the children. I respected that.

On a warm spring afternoon, I stood on the South Lawn with Secret Service Agent Bob Foster watching

Mrs. Kennedy and barefoot John-John, then about a year and a half old. John-John toddled across the lawn toward the fountain, his mother following behind. The fountain pool was full of thick sludge left over from the winter. Before anyone could get to him, John-John was up on the edge of the pool—then he was gently sliding right down into the muck.

Mrs. Kennedy went in after her little boy. She slipped and fell and then she got stuck, and neither of them could get out. Agent Foster and Head Gardener Irving Williams came to their rescue.

Bob Foster got a rope and he and I ran to the pool. We threw the rope to Mrs. Kennedy, who wrapped it around herself and John-John, and we pulled them out.

I took the First Lady and her son upstairs in the elevator. They were both absolutely filthy, covered with mud, but Mrs. Kennedy didn't seem to care. She stood and chatted with John-John as if nothing had happened. It was hard not to laugh—they looked so ridiculous.

I made friends with George Thomas, the President's valet. George wasn't a bit possessive about his boss. He was glad for any help he could get. The first time George went out for lunch, soon after the Kennedys had moved in, he came to see me in the Usher's Office.

"Bruce," said George. "Get the President up after his nap, will you? And draw his bath."

I said, "Good grief, George, what will he think when he wakes up and sees me standing there? What should I do to wake him?"

George was anxious to leave on his errand. Over his shoulder he answered, "Oh, just tickle his toes, Bruce!"

"But George," I called, after his vanishing back, "suppose the President throws something after me?"

Upstairs I drew the President's bath. I noticed that George had already laid out fresh clothes. Then I tiptoed into the President's bedroom where he and Mrs. Kennedy lay fast asleep. I stood at the end of the big bed and gingerly jiggled a presidential foot.

The President opened an eye, saw me, and didn't seem surprised.

"Hello, Bruce," he muttered groggily.

Then he jumped out of bed like a jackrabbit, took his bath, and dressed. In less than five minutes he was ready for the Oval Office. Mrs. Kennedy never stirred.

I got to know the Kennedys best in the evening hours. I remember the first time the phone rang for me in the Usher's Office after dinner. It was the President, who told me Mrs. Kennedy needed me. The First Lady was in the West Hall in her blue jeans. She asked me to help her move a sofa. Since the President couldn't lift anything because of his back, he couldn't help. He sat in an easy chair and joked, "Bruce, does your wife like to move the house around as much as Mrs. Kennedy does?" After the sofa, it was lamps, tables, chairs, and pictures that she wanted to try in different places. That was the first of many such long work nights.

I had some private times alone with the President when Mrs. Kennedy was away. Every June she took the children to Cape Cod and didn't come back back until September. President Kennedy worked late in the Oval Office when his wife was out of town. He'd come back to the second floor for his dinner at nine or ten o'clock or later.

More than any of the other presidents I knew, John F. Kennedy liked to take care of himself. He'd tell me, "Those butlers don't need to hang around waiting for me, Bruce. I'll get my own dinner. Tell them to leave it in the warming oven."

Those late evenings with the President and Mrs. Kennedy put me close to them. I became very attached to the Kennedy family. We eventually settled into a new White House routine, and the dignified quiet of the Eisenhower days faded away into the back of my mind. I had weathered my first transition. The change-over from one First Family to another is by far the toughest part of working at the White House.

One night I followed the President into the kitchen in case he needed something. He picked up a plate, sat down at the kitchen table, and dug into the food. Then he shot me a quizzical look.

"Well, Bruce, how come you're working for us Democrats?" he teased. "Are you on loan from the Republicans?"

"No, Mr. President." I kept my mouth pulled down. "I keep an open mind about politics. Who knows, I might even vote for a Democrat one of these days."

President Kennedy was right. I *was* loyal to the Republican Party. But I soon found myself on the Kennedy bandwagon. This President was super-charged, eager to bring about his "New Frontier"—a better life for Americans and peace in the world. He and most of his key aides were all restless young war veterans.

Within a hundred days of his inauguration, John F. Kennedy sent thirty-nine messages to Congress, received ten foreign leaders, held nine press conferences, and founded the Peace Corps. It seemed that luck was with him, that nothing could go wrong. These words from his inaugural address seemed like a prophesy:

"You see things and you say 'why?' But I dream things that never were; and I say 'why not?' "

But the honeymoon was soon over. Within a few months, John Kennedy was savagely attacked for the failure of the Bay of Pigs invasion. The United States backed an invasion of communist Cuba by exiles from the Castro government. The invaders were overwhelmed on the beach at the Bay of Pigs. President Kennedy shouldered all the blame for the fiasco, even though all the top military men in the country had supported the attack.

President Kennedy never again let himself be overawed by older, more experienced men. He'd respectfully ask for their opinions, but from then on he made his own final judgment.

Despite the Bay of Pigs, John Kennedy remained a very popular President. He was almost too popular. During the campaign he'd been mobbed by adoring crowds. One summer afternoon, I saw it happen at the White House.

Out on the South Lawn, President and Mrs. Kennedy stood on a small platform to greet several hundred foreign and American students. The students listened quietly behind some ropes, while Secret Service men stationed themselves along the edges of the crowd. I stood out on the South Porch in the sunshine, enjoying the President's warm and witty speech. The crowd whistled and cheered, and he grinned and waved a gay goodbye as he turned to leave.

But that crowd wouldn't give him up. They yelled

and surged forward, and the stanchions holding the rope barrier toppled over like matchsticks. The Secret Service men and White House police charged frantically through the mob to reach the President and First Lady, but their clothes were torn off their backs. Several men lost their shoes and one policeman had a heart attack on the spot.

The President's tie was snatched from around his neck, and he lost his cuff links. The students ripped open his jacket and shirt—they almost stripped him. It was a terrible sight. I was afraid they'd both be seriously hurt. The Secret Service and police finally managed to break through and make a tight circle around the President and Mrs. Kennedy. They then pushed and shoved their way backward up the steps to the South Door, and I helped get them inside. It was a great relief when I slammed the door in the face of that crazy crowd.

Mrs. Kennedy was white and shaking, but John Kennedy was cool as a cucumber. In the elevator, he looked in the mirror and said, "May I borrow your comb, Bruce?" I handed him a comb from my pocket. The President carefully combed his hair and then put *my* comb in *his* pocket. "Borrowing" my comb happened several times a week. George Thomas helpfully kept me supplied with combs.

The pressures mounted on President Kennedy. A year after the Bay of Pigs it was another crisis involving Cuba. On Monday, October 15, 1962, the President was shown aerial photos that proved Cuba was building launching pads for nuclear missiles that were en route by sea from Soviet Russia. He figured that within the week he must break this news to the American people and announce a plan to thwart the Russian–Cuban design without starting World War III.

The President organized a secret committee, called ExCom, of the most important men in his government. He then pretended to keep up a normal schedule, all the while spending the bulk of his time at the ExCom meetings. He wanted to have his plan ready before the press got wind of the missiles in Cuba.

Wednesday, Thursday, and Friday the secret meetings went on. I grew suspicious. I saw a new urgency in the way the President searched for his family every time he had a spare moment. I noticed many more newsmen about than usual.

On Saturday, rumors about Soviet weapons in Cuba hit the newspapers. Now I knew what was worrying the President. He promised the reporters he'd tell the nation about the Cuban situation on television Monday night—this gave him only forty-eight hours to decide on a plan. Never before had I seen him so grim and silent.

The final meetings of ExCom started Saturday evening in the Oval Office. I saw that room, always so neat and polished, now crowded with anxious men in shirt sleeves, plates of half-eaten sandwiches and dirty coffee cups lying about, maps unrolled on the tables and on the floor.

The butlers went home, but I stayed on. I brought fresh coffee and sandwiches to the President and his men as they struggled to find a way to get the missiles out of Cuba, short of going to war.

As the night wore on and gave way to a pale Sunday morning, I stood in the hallway outside the Oval Office hearing voices raised in loud and angry argument.

Many of the President's advisers felt that Cuba must be attacked by surprise and bombed to her knees, not only to get rid of these missiles, but to warn any future aggressors that America wouldn't tolerate a nuclear threat in her back yard. Other men claimed that the United States had no right to interfere with Cuba, especially after the Bay of Pigs. They felt that the United States must accept nuclear weapons placed nearby as other nations do.

Between these two opposite opinions there was a middle ground. Robert McNamara, Secretary of Defense, suggested a naval blockade, a line of U.S. warships with planes in support, stretching across the Carribean Sea in front of Cuba, ready to stop every Russian ship that might approach and search it for missiles.

Robert Kennedy strongly supported McNamara's plan and the President seemed to lean toward it.

At five o'clock on Monday morning, I was waiting at the elevator as President Kennedy and his brother Robert came wearily out of the Oval Office, where they had spent thirty-six straight hours in discussions. John Kennedy, his eyes red-rimmed, and his face haggard and white with exhaustion and worry, was surprised to see me there.

"Bruce! What are you doing up all night?" he asked.

"I was waiting for the President," I answered.

I took the two brothers upstairs in the elevator. They spoke of the decision that had to be made.

In a low voice, the President said, "Those trigger-happy so-and-sos want me to knock Cuba off the map. We can do that. But we'd be bullies. They could be right or they could be dead wrong."

Robert Kennedy spoke calmly. "As President, *you*

are the one who must decide. My opinion is, they're wrong. We'll get an agreement. We must be patient and stay on track."

I saw how strong and substantial a person Robert Kennedy was. He was his brother's major adviser.

The next afternoon the President's trusted aide, Ken O'Donnell, came to me in the Usher's Office with a thick brown envelope containing the President's speech for that evening. On the second floor I found the President in his dressing room and handed him the speech. John Kennedy could read almost as fast as he could turn a page. He flipped through the speech and threw it on the floor, muttering, "I've got to write my own speech."

At seven o'clock on Monday evening, President Kennedy went on nationwide TV. He told the American people about the nuclear missiles, about the Soviet "deliberate deception." He announced the plan for a naval blockade.

The President said, "The greatest danger would be to do nothing . . . our goal is not the victory of might but the vindication of right . . . both peace *and* freedom."

The U.S. Navy moved full force to blockade Cuba: ninety warships, eight huge aircraft carriers with sixty-eight plane squadrons for support. In case the worst happened, U.S. Army troops massed in Florida.

I asked myself, what would the Soviet ships do when they were blocked? Would they open fire? Would the U.S. ships and planes have to fire their guns to stop them?

At United Nations headquarters in New York City, our Ambassador Adlai Stevenson asked the other nations of the world to support our blockade. When the

Russian Ambassador denied that the Soviets had sent nuclear missiles to Cuba, Stevenson convinced the delegates by showing them the aerial photos. Soviet Premier Nikita Khrushchev was nervous. He sent roundabout messages feeling out the American government for a peaceful solution.

After another agonizing weekend, on Sunday, October 28, Khrushchev ordered his ships to turn back. Work was stopped inside Cuba. He wrote to President Kennedy:

"We should like to continue the exchange of views on the prohibition of atomic and thermonuclear weapons, general disarmament, and other problems. . . ."

President Kennedy did not crow over his victory. Instead he praised Khrushchev for his "statesmanlike decision." He was haunted by the close escape the world had had, and he felt that Khrushchev, who bore the same lonely responsibility for the lives of millions that he did, must feel the same way. The Cuban missile crisis led directly to the Nuclear Test Ban Treaty the following year.

At home in the United States, the biggest single issue facing President Kennedy was civil rights for black people. He and his brother Robert had shown their sympathy by concrete acts. In 1961, for example, a thousand Freedom Riders, black and white, went down South to challenge segregation in bus terminal restaurants, waiting rooms, and restrooms. A mob in Alabama, armed with clubs and pipes, attacked the riders, and Attorney General Robert Kennedy sent six hundred federal marshalls to quell the riot. Also the President sent federal troops to Mississippi to protect air force veteran James

Meredith, the first black to enter the University of Mississippi Law School, against defiant Governor Ross Barnett and his state troopers.

But many black people were angry; progress was too slow. Seven and a half years after *Brown* v. *Board of Education,* less than 13,000 children from all the southern states were in mixed classrooms. The right to vote was a travesty in many states, such as Mississippi, where in seventy-four out of eighty-two counties, only 15 percent of eligible blacks were allowed to register. More than twice as many blacks as whites had no jobs, nationwide—blacks were still the last hired and the first fired.

Black people took to the streets. By direct action—peaceful sit-ins, prayer-ins, marches, and boycotts—they fought for equal treatment. Mass jailings made the movement stronger. Said Martin Luther King, Jr.:

"Words cannot express the exultation felt by the individual as he finds himself, with hundreds of his fellows, behind prison bars for a cause he knows is just."

On Good Friday, April 12, 1963, Police Chief "Bull" Connor of Birmingham, Alabama, turned his snarling police dogs loose on unarmed marchers who were peacefully protesting discrimination in shops, restaurants, and employment. When horrible pictures were published of this frightful event, again the movement was strengthened.

But the more the movement grew in power, the greater was the backlash. In the deep South, some local sheriffs and police chiefs went out after black activists and illegally prosecuted them on trumped-up charges, or closed their eyes when others set out to silence them by intimidation or even murder.

Nationwide, the mood in the country was "go slow."

Congressmen and senators read their mail from the voters and became extra conservative on race. Even the Vice-President, former Senate Majority Leader Lyndon B. Johnson, could not persuade his old friends on Capitol Hill to move ahead on civil rights.

President Kennedy was blamed for encouraging the civil rights movement. In a poll, his popularity sagged from 60 percent to 47 percent. His advisers begged him to stay clear of the race issue.

Martin Luther King, Jr., too, was under heavy pressure from some of his own people. While most blacks agreed with his peaceful methods and his faith that the races would one day reconcile, others felt that he had failed—that now blacks should fight fire with fire, using violent force as racist white people did. One time in Harlem, some black people threw eggs at Martin Luther King, Jr.

Neither of these brave leaders backed down. Martin Luther King, Jr. kept his faith in non-violence. And in June 1963, President Kennedy went to Congress with his proposal for strong new civil rights laws.

The President asked Congress to end segregation nationwide in all public places, and to give the Attorney General the power to sue on behalf of black children to open up white schools. He also wanted fair employment programs and improved voting laws.

Martin Luther King, Jr. and other civil rights leaders decided on a big march and a siege on the U.S. Capitol to pressure the congressmen and senators to pass John Kennedy's new Civil Rights Bill into law.

The President was worried about the planned march. He feared that certain lawmakers, who hadn't yet made up their minds to vote "yes," would get angry at a crowd of black people besieging the Capitol. That might give them an excuse to vote "no." So John Kennedy called the leaders of the march to the White House to talk it over. He hoped to persuade them to put off the march until sometime later.

On June 22, 1963, I met the top black leaders of the United States at the North Door of the White House and took them into the Red Room to wait for the President.

There was Whitney Young of the Urban League, James Farmer of the Congress of Racial Equality, Roy Wilkins and Clarence Mitchell, veterans of so many battles of the National Association for the Advancement of Colored People, the venerable A. Phillip Randolph, long-time head of the Brotherhood of Sleeping Car Porters, Bayard Rustin, organizer of the march, and of course, Martin Luther King, Jr.

In the Red Room, A. Phillip Randolph, Whitney Young, and Clarence Mitchell came up to me and we talked for fifteen minutes. They wanted to know if, in my personal opinion, John F. Kennedy was a fair and sincere man. Or was he just another false politician saying things he didn't really mean? I told them I had had only fair treatment from the President and that I believed both he and his brother cared heart and soul about justice for black people.

The President personally escorted the black leaders to the Cabinet Room for the meeting.

Later President Kennedy's resident historian, Arthur Schlesinger, Jr. said, "It was the best meeting I attended in my years at the White House."

John F. Kennedy said, "We want success in Congress, not just a big show at the Capitol."

A. Phillip Randolph said, "The Negroes are already in the streets; it is very likely impossible to get them off . . . is it not better that they be led by organizations dedicated to civil rights and disciplined by struggle rather than to leave them to other leaders who care neither about civil rights nor about non-violence?"

Martin Luther King, Jr. said that though the march might seem to the President to be "ill-timed," yet "Frankly, I have never engaged in any direct action movement which did not seem ill-timed." He felt the march "could also serve as a means of dramatizing the issue and mobilizing support in parts of the country which don't know the problems at first hand. I think it will serve a purpose."

The President gracefully accepted the decision of the black leaders to go ahead with their march. He said, "This is a very serious fight. . . . What is important is that we preserve confidence in the good faith of each other. I have my problems with the Congress: You have yours with your own groups. We will undoubtedly disagree from time to time on tactics. But the important thing is to keep in touch."

After the White House meeting, the black leaders announced that a demonstration would take place at the Lincoln Memorial rather than a siege of the U.S. Capitol. President Kennedy announced his full support to this "peaceful assembly . . . in the great tradition." Now, he felt, the lawmakers on Capitol Hill couldn't complain they were being threatened.

On the historic date of August 28, 1963, nearly a quar-

ter of a million people came to the Lincoln Memorial
in Washington, D.C. Black and white, men, women,
and children; they arrived by car, by bus, by plane, and
on foot. Martin Luther King, Jr. made his never-to-be-
forgotten speech:

"I still have a dream. . . . I have a dream that on the
red hills of Georgia the sons of former slaves and the
sons of former slaveowners will be able to sit together
at the table of brotherhood. . . . I have a dream that
even the state of Mississippi, a state sweltering with the
heat of injustice, will be transformed into an oasis of
freedom. . . ."

That afternoon, John Kennedy left his Oval Office
early. He asked me to go to the third floor Solarium
with him.

The President and I stood together at the Solarium
window. We couldn't see the crowd over the treetops
but we heard its one great voice:

> "We shall overcome, we shall overcome,
> We shall overcome, some day.
> Oh deep in my heart, I do believe
> We shall overcome some day."

John Kennedy gripped the window sill, his knuckles
white. His voice choked as he said, "Oh, Bruce, I wish
I were out there with them!"

The new civil rights laws were passed by Congress
the following February, but President John F. Kennedy
would not share in the triumph.

In October, congressmen and senators left Washington for their home districts. President Kennedy, too, wanted to check the mood of the country. The feedback, the warmth from the crowds nourished him. He liked best to wade out into the middle of a big crowd, using his shoulders like a football player to make his way, while people tugged at his sleeve and slapped his back. Along a parade route, he refused the safe bullet-proof closed limousine that the Secret Service begged him to use. Instead, he liked an open car. He'd sit high on top of the back seat, where he could meet the eyes of the people and hear their greetings in the open air as he waved to them. John Kennedy wanted to stay as close as possible to the people who had given him the job of President.

A big trip to Texas was planned for late November, with stops at San Antonio, Houston, Dallas, and Austin. One evening, about a week before the trip to Texas, I met the President and Mrs. Kennedy at the South Door of the White House as they returned from a quiet dinner with old friends. They were being very affectionate together, so I walked ahead of them on the way to the elevator to give them some privacy. I heard Mrs. Kennedy say something very unusual, in a voice so soft I could barely make out her words.

"Jack," she asked, "do you have to go on this trip to Dallas? I don't want you to go."

The President sounded surprised as he answered, "It's all set up, Jackie. I've promised. Of course I must go."

"Please don't go, Jack," she said insistently.

Kindly but firmly the President repeated, "There's no way I can back out, Jackie. Will you come too? I want you to go with me."

Mrs. Kennedy was silent. She rarely went on political trips. But something seemed to be tugging at her. She decided to go to Texas with her husband.

On the morning of Thursday, November 21, 1963, I brought Mrs. Kennedy down from the second floor. She was ready to leave for Texas and she looked beautiful. The President walked over from the Oval Office to join her. He was buoyant, glad to be getting out of Washington and happy that his wife was going with him.

I stood with the Kennedys out on the South Portico as the big army helicopter revved up its engines. The President patted me on the shoulder.

"Now, Bruce," he said, mock serious, "I'm leaving you in charge of everything here. You run things to suit yourself!"

"Yes, I certainly will, Mr. President," I answered. But for all the joking, it gave me a pang to see the helicopter disappear from sight through the big trees overhead.

Around one o'clock on the afternoon of Friday, November 22, my wife and I were having a fish lunch together in our kitchen. Music was playing from the small radio on the table. Suddenly the shrill voice of an announcer broke into the program:

"We have an important announcement from Dallas, Texas. The President has been shot!"

To this day I can still feel the shock that ran through my whole body at these words. I cracked my knee on the table as I jumped up from my chair. Grabbing my coat, I rushed from the house, got in my car, and took off down the street.

As I hit 16th Street, I was going fifty-five miles an hour in city traffic. I heard a policeman's siren behind me and pulled over. I didn't even think to pull out my White House ID card.

"Officer," I blurted, "I work at the White House. The President has been shot."

The officer believed me. "C'mon," he called as he jumped back on his motorcycle, "follow me!"

The motorcycle careened up 16th Street, with me following, until we reached the sentry box at the Southwest Gate of the White House, where I was waved onto the grounds.

It was Tuesday, November 26th, four days later, before I again passed through the White House gate on my way home.

We got the news at two o'clock that afternoon that the President was dead. Lee Harvey Oswald had shot John Kennedy as he smiled and waved to the crowds along the parade route in Dallas. Oswald had placed himself high above the parade route at a warehouse window. He had hidden behind a carefully positioned stack of cardboard cartons and lain in wait for the President to come within the telescopic sight of his rifle.

I was completely numb. There was only one idea in my mind. I would wait for Mrs. Kennedy. I wanted to be there when she came back to the White House.

The hours passed. Mrs. Kennedy sent word that she wanted the White House to look just as it had for the funeral of President Abraham Lincoln after he had been assassinated.

Everyone pitched in to help. We draped yards and yards of black crepe all over the first floor reception rooms. It was strange to be up on a ladder, side by side with the girls from the Social Office, Jerry Whittington from the Press Office, and so many others.

Sergeant Shriver, whose wife Eunice was John Kennedy's sister, took charge and other family members came to take his orders. The way the Kennedy family pulled together was magnificent.

A huge high bier, called a catafalque, on which the President's casket was to rest, was brought from the U.S. Capitol. The bodies of three other Presidents slain by assassins had lain on it. Charles Ficklen, the maître d', and I each carried in a giant taper and placed it next to the bier.

At last, at four in the morning, after most of the worn-out staff had left, I heard police sirens outside the White House. I went to the North Door as the black hearse drove up the driveway. Inside the hearse I saw the outlines of the casket. My heart pounded; how could my President be lying there just hours after we had joked together on the South Portico? He hadn't even lived yet.

Mrs. Kennedy, leaning on Robert Kennedy, climbed the steps slowly, her pink suit stained with her husband's blood. At the top she saw me. She seemed terrifyingly calm, her eyes huge, her small face dead white.

"Bruce, you waited until we came." Her voice was so kind, as if she wanted to comfort me.

"Yes, you knew I was going to be here, Mrs. Kennedy," I said.

Charles Ficklen and I lit the candles next to the bier. After a short mass, Mrs. Kennedy put her head down on the flag that covered the coffin.

Poor Robert Kennedy, dazed with grief, guided Mrs. Kennedy to the elevator, where I was waiting for them. As the door closed and we started to move, I couldn't hold back my tears any longer. Robert Kennedy and

Mrs. Kennedy put their arms around me and we wept together in the elevator as it traveled up to the second floor.

As dawn broke on Saturday, November 23rd, I sat upright in a chair in a small third floor bedroom at the White House. I'd taken off my jacket and tie and opened my stiff white collar, but I didn't want to lie down, in case Mrs. Kennedy needed me. My mind went around in circles. How could God have let this happen?

I knew the whole world was grieving. The leader of Guinea, a small country in Africa, said, "I have lost my only true friend in the outside world." Bells tolled in Poland. Streets and schools all over South America were almost immediately named for John F. Kennedy. Behind the Iron Curtain in Yugoslavia, tough Marshall Tito could hardly speak when he telephoned U.S. officials to express his sorrow. In Germany, Berliners darkened their houses and put lighted candles in their windows in honor of the slain American President.

Like me, people everywhere mourned John Kennedy as a friend as well as a leader. His youthful hope for a better world had been contagious. Now people felt their hopes die with him.

I felt in my heart that, though his time as President had been cruelly cut short, John F. Kennedy had made a difference. He'd earned new goodwill toward the United States from countries around the world. He had persuaded the Soviet Union to sign the Nuclear Test Ban Treaty. He had created the Peace Corps, a symbol of a new spirit of caring in American foreign policy. And he had encouraged the black people at home to make solid gains in their struggle for fair treatment. It helped me to remember these deeds as I moved through the nightmare weekend.

Starting at ten o'clock Saturday morning, I helped to receive the dignitaries who came in a steady stream all day long to pass by the bier and pay their last respects to the fallen President. Many of these people remembered me from happier days and greeted me with sympathy.

Just before midnight, the East Room was closed to visitors.

I brought Mrs. Kennedy downstairs. She wanted time alone near her husband's body before the casket was moved to the Capitol. There it would remain until the burial on Monday.

All day Sunday, November 24th, thousands upon thousands of Americans, young, old, rich, poor, black, white, Republicans, and Democrats, said goodbye to John F. Kennedy at the Capitol.

On that Sunday, we at the White House worked hard. After the funeral on Monday at Arlington Cemetery, the new President, Lyndon B. Johnson, would receive at the White House all the world leaders who had traveled to America for the funeral. There would be more heads of state assembled under one roof than ever before in history.

That day was completely unlike any that I had ever been through at the White House. The atmosphere was one of complete sadness. As we worked, we didn't talk unless it was absolutely necessary. Everybody was just filled up.

It was the same outside the White House. The sidewalks around the mansion, and Lafayette Square across

Pennsylvania Avenue, were filled with people, silently gazing at the White House, too sad to speak to each other.

I looked out the window at this eerie sight, this silent crowd. There was little for them to see. Perhaps, I thought, just the sight of the mansion, still standing solid despite this disaster, somehow reassured them that America would pull through.

Early Monday morning, I was waiting near the elevator when Usher Rex Scouten came to find me. "Come to the office immediately," he said, "the Attorney General is looking for you."

I met Robert Kennedy. "Bruce," he said, "Mrs. Kennedy and the family want you to walk with us to the church. Then someone will drive you to the cemetery.

In the chill morning air, I walked behind the Kennedy family to Saint Matthews Cathedral. My heart ached to see Mrs. Kennedy march up the avenue, straight-backed, holding her children by the hand. She held her head high, underneath a heavy mourning veil of deep black, as she led the sorrowful procession.

Behind the flag-draped casket, mounted on an artillery caisson pulled by six beautiful white horses, was Black Jack, the riderless black stallion. Two empty high black boots were turned backward in his stirrups.

The restless horse pranced and reared, while bagpipers, dear to John Kennedy's heart, played a mournful lament.

The Cathedral Service went by like a dream. Afterward, I stood at the bottom of the steps near Mrs.

Kennedy, Caroline, and John-John as the pallbearers carried down the casket. As it passed by, John-John raised his small hand and gave a crisp salute. It was his third birthday, and his mother had arranged ice cream, cake, and candles to go with his supper that evening.

McGeorge Bundy, the President's National Security Advisor, asked me to ride with him and Mrs. Bundy to Arlington Cemetery in their car. I knew and liked the Bundys and was glad to ride with them, but it was incredible to me that the Kennedys had found time to arrange this for me.

I stood on the hillside at Arlington. In every direction I saw line upon line of plain white crosses, marking the graves of American soldiers. Around me were members of the Kennedy family, their close friends, and dignitaries. I came close to breaking down again, but I struggled to keep my composure. I could see the head of tall somber General Charles de Gaulle of France, in his splendid military cap, just a few feet away, and I could have reached out and touched Emperor Haile Selassie of Ethiopia. Mrs. Kennedy had done me a great honor to include me in this company.

At last the bugle sounded taps for John Fitzgerald Kennedy, a brave young man I'd learned to love.

# Chapter 4

# THE JOHNSONS

ON December 7, 1963, President Lyndon Johnson and his family moved into the White House, which was still draped in black after John Kennedy's funeral less than three weeks before. I had known Lyndon Johnson for a long time. As Majority Leader of the Senate, he'd often been invited by President Eisenhower to discuss civil rights and other matters. Then as Vice-President to President Kennedy, he'd been present at many private meetings in the family quarters upstairs. I had heard of his bad temper, but he'd always been cordial to me.

The contrast was startling between John Kennedy, Harvard graduate and son of multi-millionaire Ambassador Joseph P. Kennedy, and Lyndon B. Johnson, born on a parched ranch in the harsh and poor flatlands of central Texas, a country of fearful droughts, scorching summer heat, and terrifying winter blizzards.

John F. Kennedy spoke with grace and charm, while Lyndon Johnson's speech was often crude and earthy. President Johnson's moods were as changeable as the weather of his native state.

The day President Johnson moved into the White House, he gave a reception for more than two hundred people on the second floor. He wanted to bring together his own personal staff and all the Kennedy staff people who were still there. It was unheard of to have such a big party in the family quarters. It made extra work for the butlers to haul all the food and drink up there. I was the only doorman on duty, and I had to be three places at once all day. It was a long, hard day and my nerves were still raw from the shock of the assassination.

Guests straggled out slowly. They lingered at the South Door, talking on and on. I hurried back to the elevator so I could bring down more people. To my surprise I saw the elevator light blinking and blinking in a way that could mean only one thing. The President was calling for the elevator.

The moment the elevator door opened upstairs, there was big, tall Lyndon B. Johnson. His craggy face was beet red and he seemed to fill up the whole doorway. He bore down on me, yelling at the top of his lungs, "Where have you been? I've been *waiting* and *waiting* for this elevator!" He stuck out his chest and stomach and moved in on me as if he would run me right over. I had to decide in a split second whether or not to back off and move out of his way.

I was furious. I was just as keyed up as he was and I was the wrong person for him to take it out on. I didn't move an inch and I looked right into his eyes. With a funny, surprised look on his face, he stepped to one side, awkwardly.

I kept calm while he went on roaring and raging.

"Mr. President," I said, "I've been trying to get your guests out of the house. I know how to do it, but I must have time."

President Johnson cooled down somewhat and growled, "If you don't have someone to help, tell them to hire someone!"

"Well, Mr. President," I answered back coldly, "if *you* call the Usher's Office, I'm sure they'll be delighted to do that."

All this time the President's guests, Congressman and Mrs. Jack Brooks and President Kennedy's trusted aides, Ted Sorenson and Ken O'Donnell, were standing by in stunned silence. I took them downstairs and showed them out of the White House.

Then I went into the Usher's Office, seething with rage.

"I will not work here any longer, being treated like this!" I told my good friend, Usher Nelson Pierce. "Furthermore, I'm never going to get over President Kennedy's death. I'm going now."

Nelson helped me to calm down and told me to go home and sleep on it. He was very worried I would either quit or be fired.

The next morning I went up to Capitol Hill to talk to friends there about another job. In the afternoon I came on duty at the White House and waited in the Usher's Office for the signal that the President was coming back from his Oval Office. I just knew he and I were in for a big fight that night. If he didn't want me there, this is going to be it, I decided.

When President Johnson came through the door from the West Wing, he yelled out, "Well, here's my old friend Bruce? Howya doin' Bruce? Howdya feel tonight?"

I stood straight and answered, "I'm fine, Mr. President. I hope you're feeling well."

"Yes, yes, I'm feeling all right. You know, Bruce, we're going to get along fine!" he intoned.

"Thank you, Mr. President. I certainly hope so," I said.

But inside I was thinking, I doubt I will *ever* get along with this man.

When we got upstairs, the President got off the elevator and tapped me on the shoulder.

"Thank you, Bruce," he said to me. Then he repeated, "I know we're going to get along just all right."

Downstairs the ushers were amazed. One of them said, "Golly, I can't believe it! After the way he sounded off last night!"

For sometime after that, I made sure to answer President Johnson in a very stern and know-how manner. It was obvious to me that if I started scraping and bowing when he lost his temper, that would be the end of me. If he thought he could yell at me any time he felt like it, the way he did to many others—including some in very high positions—I'd have had to quit my job. President or not, I would not stand for rude treatment. President Johnson never raised his voice to me again, but that was only the first of many hurdles. Getting used to President Johnson's White House was tough.

Lyndon B. Johnson was the hardest working man I've ever seen in my life. He'd done a normal day's work, upstairs in his bedroom, by ten o'clock in the morning, plowing through five or ten pounds of paper, all the while keeping one eye peeled on his television console with three screens—one for each network.

President Johnson went to the Oval Office mid-morning and he might come back for lunch at one, two, or three—you never knew. He took an hour's nap from four to five, then I'd take him downstairs to go back to the office. He'd stay there until anywhere from eight to nine o'clock to as late as midnight or one o'clock in the morning. He'd bring five or six people back from the office with him for late supper. By the time he went to bed, I'd be getting away from the White House at two o'clock in the morning.

When the President came back late at night from the office, I'd be waiting for him at the elevator. He'd act surprised, saying,

"What are you doing up so late, Bruce? Why are you here?"

That was some kind of joke—I *had* to be there. If no one had been there, there'd be a hole right through the ceiling. If it was four in the morning, somebody had to be there. He expected it and he got it.

The last straw was that two or three times a month the President flew to his beloved Texas, and he'd get back to the White House at four in the morning or later. That was killing me; I couldn't stand it.

So I asked to take the morning shift. Then I had to be at the White House at 6:30 A.M., but at least my hours were regular. Two or three times a week I stayed for functions and worked a double shift.

The new First Lady, tiny dark-haired Lady Bird Johnson, who hardly came up to her husband's shoulder, was another hard worker. I never saw her take a moment for herself all the time she was at the White House. If she didn't have anything planned, the Social Office would manufacture something to get her going again. I often thought, "Can't they let her rest for a little while?" Unlike Mrs. Kennedy, Lady Bird Johnson never said "No."

The Johnsons had more dinners, luncheons, and receptions in one year than the Kennedys and Eisenhowers together did in all the years they were in office. It was rough for all of us who worked there—some days we didn't know how we were going to make it.

One day the President phoned Chief Usher J. B. West from Capitol Hill at two o'clock in the afternoon. He'd just invited the entire Congress, their wives and families, to the White House that evening. We took care of one thousand unexpected guests that night.

The Social Office would plan events back to back, and that was very awkward. The military aides on the ground floor would be trying to pacify incoming guests, while I was upstairs trying to move another group out the door. I'd have to practically push people out—nobody wants to leave the White House. People won't be hurried and I don't blame them.

The president's two teenage daughters, Lynda Bird and Luci Baines, were part of the Johnson political team. As soon as they moved in, they went to work to lighten the load on their mother and father. They met all the school groups and told them what it was like to live in the White House. I helped the young women to

111

handle these groups, and we soon became fond of each other.

The Johnson girls and their mother idolized the President. I never saw Lady Bird when she wasn't glad to see her darling. "My darling!" That's what she always called him.

One time Lynda was buzzing for the elevator and she found out that Mr. Harriston had it on hold for the President. Lynda walked up the steps and said to Mr. Harriston, "What are you doing? Are you holding the elevator for God?"

She made it into a joke, but to her and her sister and her mother, the President *was* God Almighty. And Lyndon Johnson returned their love. Every time he came back from the Oval Office he'd ask me where each one of them was, and I had to have the answers.

No matter how hard we all tried, Lyndon B. Johnson couldn't be kept happy. He was like a volcano, liable to erupt at any moment.

One day I was up on the second floor waiting for the President. He was in his bedroom talking to one of his closest aides, Marvin Watson. I'd been there for over an hour, and I badly needed to go to the men's room. I thought they'd be in there for a while longer.

I made a mad dash downstairs, where I locked the elevator on hold so no one could take it away from me. That way I could rush right back upstairs in case President Johnson got ready to move.

I'd no sooner left with the elevator than the President wanted it. He called the Usher's Office and roared, "Get me the elevator!"

Orville Liser ran down to the basement, grabbed the

elevator, and took it up to the second floor. There the roof fell in on him.

The President yelled so loudly that I could hear him down in the basement. "You lazy SOB, how dare you take my elevator. Don't you know I'm the President?" Poor Liser never had a chance to say he hadn't taken the elevator.

Liser came down to the basement in a state of shock. When he saw me, he gasped, "Bruce, did you hear him?"

"People must have heard him across Pennsylvania Avenue," I said.

"Oh, did he raise Cain!" Liser said. "He took the ceiling off! I never even had a chance to tell him I didn't do it."

"Well, I will tell him," I said.

"He told Mr. Watson to find out who it was and fire him!"

"I locked it," I said.

"Oh, no!" Liser shook his head sympathetically.

I went to the Usher's Office, and one of the Secret Service men there said, "Bruce, do you know who locked the elevator? Mr. Watson told me the President said to find out who it was and *fire* him!"

"*I* am the one who locked it."

"But I have to tell the President," he said.

"Fine!" I said. "You tell whoever you have to."

He said, "Can't you say you don't know who—you left it and somebody else brought it down and locked it?"

"No," I said, "I can't say that because I *did*. It'll be all right. I'll call Marvin Watson. You go on over to the Oval Office and tell him you found the man."

So I picked up the phone. Marvin Watson took my call.

I said, "Mr. Watson, I apologize for having to bother you now. I know you are busy, but I still want to say that I'm sorry I was the one who locked the elevator." And I told him why.

"Oh, Bruce," he said, "I kind of felt you were the one. Listen, you forget it. I'll explain to the President."

That evening, I met the President when he came back from the office.

"Ohhhh! Bruce," he said. "What were you trying to do? Make me have a heart attack?"

"No, Mr. President, and I'm sorry the elevator wasn't there when you needed it."

I didn't really think the President would fire me. He had fired Secret Service men a couple of times a week because he hated to have them around, then the next day he told them what a good job they were doing. I wasn't too worried, but it was a little tense.

He was a different President when his two daughters got married. They were both beautiful brides. Those were the only times I ever saw Lyndon B. Johnson when he didn't know exactly what he was going to do next. He took orders like a docile little boy.

Luci Baines was the first married, to Patrick Nugent on May 6, 1966. She was the President's baby, the one who could twist him around her little finger. All during the reception at the White House the newsmen and photographers tried to find out when the bride and groom would leave and where they were going. No one knew except the chauffeur who would drive them, the Secret Service, Chief Usher J. B. West, and me. I was the one to sneak them out, and that was fun! I put them

on the freight elevator and took them through the
kitchens and out to a little Plymouth that was waiting
for them. A big limousine stood ready on the other side
of the house to throw the newsmen off the scent. Everyone was still waiting for Luci and Pat on the south
grounds when they were halfway to Pennsylvania! As I
put Luci in the Plymouth, she gave me a big smack on
the cheek.

Lynda's groom, Charles Robb, was a favorite of mine.
He was the Marine Color Guard Captain, and I'd
helped to break him in when he first came into the
White House.

We decorated the Grand Stairway with yellow and
white roses for Lynda. When President Johnson
brought her down the stairs it was plain that he was a
proud father. But family events were few and far between in the Johnson White House. Lyndon B. Johnson
was determined to make his place in history.

President Johnson burned to finish all of John
Kennedy's work and to push through his own program,
"The Great Society." He wanted to abolish poverty and
unemployment, to encourage business, and perfect the
schools. Two hundred twenty-six new laws that President Johnson wanted were passed by the Congress in
four years. That was a record.

The new President's very first priority was John
Kennedy's Civil Rights Bill. Lyndon Johnson's devotion
to civil rights was deep. His own father, Sam Ealy Johnson, had stood against the Klu Klux Klan in the Texas
legislature. He'd barely escaped being tarred and feath-
ered. As a boy, Lyndon Johnson had grown up with the
fear that his daddy might be hurt by racial bigots.

Young Lyndon Johnson had been director of the National Youth Administration in Texas, which gave jobs to young people out of work during the Great Depression. Of Johnson's work in those days, a black leader has said, "We began to get word up here that there was one NYA director who wasn't like the others. He was looking after Negroes and poor folks and most NYA people weren't doing that."

While President Kennedy was alive, most people expected only a watered down verson of his Civil Rights Bill to pass the Congress, because the southern leaders would "filibuster," or talk it to death. Under Senate rules, a senator can talk forever unless two thirds of the Senate votes "cloture"—to close off further talk on a subject.

Having been Majority Leader in the Senate, Lyndon B. Johnson knew how lawmakers think and feel. He was a great tactician, a master arm-twister, superb at face-to-face persuasion. He set out to earn support for the Civil Rights Act of 1964.

I saw the whole thing break wide open in the White House. The President would summon senators and congressmen to visit with him upstairs in the family quarters. He'd give the lawmakers a couple of cocktails and hors d'oeuvres. Then he'd get down to business. He'd tempt and he'd threaten. The senators would get favors —juicy projects for their states that would make them very popular with the voters—*if* they cooperated. If they didn't, he'd cut them off at the pockets. Not a penny of federal money would come their way.

When the President got steamed up, he'd swear like a trooper at those important men. I heard him do it.

He'd be like an army drill sergeant with a bunch of green recruits. He got away with it because he was the President.

The men I took downstairs in the elevator after those sessions would sometimes be absolutely furious. But the President got results. He never attacked his opponents in the press, but he'd hammer them in private. He believed that if you talk *to* somebody, you have a better chance to get what you want than if you talk *at* them.

President Johnson sent his top aides, men like Jack Valenti, all over Capitol Hill to talk to senators and congressmen. He coached these aides on how to treat the powerful politicians. One day, I was amazed to hear him talk about me at one of these coaching sessions.

He said, "You can model yourselves after Mr. Bruce, there. He always has dignity, he's a man that you can't push around, but he always treats you with great courtesy and respect. It's as if he's saying to you that I'm going to pay *you* the same kind of courtesy and respect that I expect you to pay *me.* And so that's how I want you to treat these senators and congressmen."

The key to President Johnson's strategy to get the Civil Rights Act passed was the powerful Republican Senator, Everett B. Dirksen, a man I knew and liked. He came to the White House so often in those days, he used to say, "Bruce, you must think I live here."

Senator Dirksen was tall, with a big head of curly white hair, and a mobile face that made you smile. He'd puff away on his pipe. Some people called him the "the wizard of ooze" because of his silky smooth voice. He always embraced me and called me his dear friend.

President Johnson knew he must have Republican

votes to defeat a filibuster in the Senate and get the Civil Rights Act passed. He needed Senator Dirksen to line up his Republican friends.

First, Lyndon Johnson persuaded his own black friends, Roy Wilkins, head of the NAACP, and Whitney Young, president of the Urban League, to work on Everett Dirksen. The black leaders convinced the wily Senator that the Republican Party would reap a harvest of black votes in future elections if he and his fellow Republicans put across the Civil Rights Act. This was the party of Abraham Lincoln, after all.

Then the President himself wooed and flattered Senator Dirksen. For this man Lyndon Johnson used honey, not the big stick. Everett Dirksen's mood would be wonderful as he rode down with me in the elevator after his visits with the President.

On June 10, 1964, Dirksen led a group of senators voting for cloture to stop the southern filibuster. And at the White House, on July 2, President Johnson signed the Civil Rights Act of 1964.

Next President Johnson asked his Attorney General to draft a new Voting Rights Act for the Congress, while at the same time, Martin Luther King, Jr. started his all-out drive to register southern black voters. On March 7, 1965, he led a protest march from Selma to Montgomery, Alabama. Governor Wallace sent state police to break up the march. They beat the unarmed marchers with their billy clubs. Demonstrations multiplied and the reactions grew more and more violent until President Johnson sent federal troops to Alabama. Then he speeded up action on the Voting Rights Bill.

President Johnson presented his bill to Congress in a nighttime joint session of Congress at the U.S. Capitol.

All the TV networks showed the President giving the finest speech of his political life.

I watched the President as he said:

"What happened in Selma is part of a far larger movement. . . . It is the effort of American Negroes to secure for themselves the full blessings of American life. Their cause must be our cause too. Because it is not just Negroes, but really it is all of us who must overcome the crippling legacy of bigotry and injustice."

Then the President stopped, raised his arms and repeated, "And . . . we . . . shall . . . overcome."

An observer told of the response to the President's words, "The whole chamber was on its feet. . . . In the galleries Negroes and whites, some in rumpled sports shirts of bus rides from the demonstrations, others in trim professional suits, wept unabashedly."

Then President Johnson recalled the days when he was a young teacher in the town of Cotulla, Texas:

"Somehow you never forget what poverty and hatred can do when you see its scars on the hopeful face of a young child. I never thought then, in 1928, that I would be standing here in 1965. It never occurred to me in my fondest dreams that I might have the chance to help. . . . But now I do have that chance—I'll let you in on a secret—I mean to use it. . . . I want to be the President who educated young children . . . who helped to feed the hungry . . . who helped the poor to find their own way and who protected the right of every citizen to vote in every election. . . ."

The next morning at the White House, I said to President Johnson, "Mr. President, that was a wonderful speech you gave last night. It moved me so much, I wanted to tell you about it."

He seemed pleased. He must have known that I spoke from the heart.

President Johnson's Voting Rights Bill speeded through Congress. Many black people in the South now dared to vote for the first time. But the new civil rights laws had little or no effect on the lives of desperately poor and jobless black people in the crowded ghettos of the North.

Only a few days after Lyndon B. Johnson signed the Voting Rights Act, a terrible riot broke out in Watts, a suburb of Los Angeles. This was the first in a series of riots in northern cities over three summers that left 225 people dead, 4,000 wounded, and destroyed $112 billion worth of property.

Martin Luther King, Jr. joined with those who criticized the President, saying he wasn't doing enough to help the poor people in the ghettos. That enraged the President and he talked to me about it.

We were in the elevator. President Johnson looked through the bottom of his glasses at me and said, "Bruce, do you think I am doing all I can for black people?"

"Yes, I do, Mr. President," I answered, "unless there is some way you can go inside each person's mind and change that."

"Well, damn it, did you read what Martin Luther King, Jr. just said about me?" he asked.

The President was so angry, I believe he would have punched Martin Luther King, Jr. if he'd been there with us.

I answered, "Yes, I read all that, Mr. President, but I don't agree with him. I wish he knew as much about what you've done as I do."

The President said, "Thanks, Bruce. You are one of the dearest friends I have."

The President was crushed at the anger black people felt toward him, yet he understood it. Later he said, "As I see it, I've moved the Negro from D plus to C minus. He's still nowhere. He knows it."

The President had made a start on the root causes of the riots in his war on poverty programs and massive aid to education. If only he could have continued to concentrate his immense energies on these things, I believe he could have made real headway. That masterful, dynamic man could have done almost anything he set his mind to.

Instead, the fate of a small country in Southeast Asia, Vietnam, distracted President Johnson's attention. From there on, the Johnson Presidency was dominated by Vietnam. Progress at home ground to a halt.

Ever since 1954, when the French were defeated by Vietnamese guerrillas at Dien Bien Phu, the small Indochinese countries of Vietnam, Laos, and Cambodia were a cause of worry for every President and the American people. Following the spectacular U.S. victories of World War II, the Communist conquest of China in 1949 was a shock. During the 1950's, politicians argued over who "lost" China, as if it had ever been "ours," and many Americans feared all of Asia would go "Red." Proud of the success of Presidents Truman and Eisenhower in using NATO to contain European Communism behind the "Iron Curtain," many Americans wanted a similar order established in Asia.

Combat commanders, including General Douglas MacArthur, leader of the Allied Forces in the Southwest Pacific during World War II and later in Korea, and General Matthew B. Ridgeway, MacArthur's successor, repeatedly warned against bogging down U.S. troops in any land war in Asia. General Charles de Gaulle, from the bitter experience of the French surrender at Dien Bien Phu, echoed these warnings.

On the other hand, a large number of distinguished generals and admirals at the Pentagon, as well as important civilian officials at the State Department and elsewhere, argued for a heavy American military effort in Indochina. They were certain, and they so persuaded many Americans, that it would be dangerous to our security to allow any part of Indochina to go Communist.

In 1954, the Geneva Conference divided Vietnam into two parts: North Vietnam, where Ho Chi Minh was the Communist leader, and South Vietnam.

By 1959, at the end of President Eisenhower's term of office, the governments of both Laos and South Vietnam were seriously threatened by Communist revolutionary movements. President Diem of South Vietnam was corrupt and hated by his people. Two percent of the people owned forty-five percent of the land. In Laos, the pro-American government was fast losing ground to the Pathet Lao, who was supported by the Soviet Union.

Despite strong urgings from ex-President Eisenhower, the new President, John F. Kennedy, fresh from the humiliation of the Bay of Pigs, refused to intervene in Laos. Instead he started negotiations with Russia to neutralize that country.

Vietnam, however, was different. A quarter of a million Vietnamese were under arms, while the Communist Viet Cong had only twelve thousand guerillas. A moderate amount of U.S. help might stave off the Communists and keep South Vietnam firmly pro-American. The generals and admirals at the Pentagon asked President Kennedy for 3,600 combat troops for Vietnam. In the spring of 1961, John F. Kennedy, with grave misgivings, for he was fully aware of the warnings of MacArthur, Ridgway, De Gaulle and others, agreed to send one hundred military advisers and four hundred Green Berets. His Vice-President, Lyndon B. Johnson, whom he had just sent to Vietnam, had no such doubts. He wanted maximum support for President Diem, whom he compared to Winston Churchill. Though widely praised for sending military help to South Vietnam, John Kennedy himself was uncomfortable. He told historian Arthur Schlesinger: "The troops will march in; the crowds will cheer; and in four days everyone will have forgotten. Then we will be told that we have to send in more troops. It is like taking a drink. The effect wears off, and you have to take another."

This was the fatal beginning. During the three-year Kennedy Presidency, the South Vietnamese government under Diem grew weaker and more corrupt until it was overthrown and Diem himself was killed in early November of 1963, about two weeks before John Kennedy, too, was assassinated. All the while, the North Vietnamese Communists grew in strength, and the pressure mounted on President Kennedy to escalate U.S. involvement. Little by little, he compromised. When Lyndon Johnson took over as President, there were seventeen thousand military advisers in Vietnam, and seventy-three American soldiers were dead.

In November 1963, just before his death, John Kennedy had in hand a plan to get all the Americans out of Vietnam by 1965, *after* the 1964 Presidential election, when he had hoped to be re-elected. He knew that many Americans did not share his wish to pull out of Vietnam. A few months earlier, a midsummer poll had shown that Americans 2 to 1 favored sending troops to Vietnam "on a large scale."

President Truman, on his own authority, had fought a large-scale war in Korea, using Presidential power, leftover from World War II, to draft young men into the Army. But time and again, President Kennedy said he didn't believe a President had the right to send combat troops into battle without first getting from Congress a Declaration of War, as required by the Constitution.

As long as he lived, John Kennedy steadfastly refused to send combat troops to Vietnam, or to bomb North Vietnam, despite heavy pressure from the Pentagon and also from many of his own closest advisers—Secretary of Defense Robert McNamara, National Security Advisor McGeorge Bundy, Secretary of State Dean Rusk, and many others.

The new President, Lyndon Johnson, on the contrary, was in harmony with the Pentagon and his cabinet, including McNamara, Bundy, and Rusk. Victory in Vietnam, not withdrawal, was his aim. At first he was cautious. Up for re-election in 1964, he said he would never send American boys to fight wars that Asian boys should fight for themselves. But in 1965, after his landslide re-election victory, he began to move. The "Red Menace" in Asia became very real to Lyndon B. Johnson.

President Johnson chose to escalate slowly. He sent bombers and combat troops in relatively small batches, so as not to alarm the country. He did not call up the

Army and Navy reserves, a public act signaling war. Instead, he quietly increased the size of draft calls. He never asked the Congress to declare war.

By July 1965, two hundred thousand American combat troops were in Vietnam. When the President asked the Senate for seven hundred million dollars to support those men, only three senators voted "no." This mirrored the feelings of Americans around the nation who felt that, once committed, our troops deserved this support.

But as the months of 1965 and 1966 passed by, victory slipped away. The more U.S. troops were poured into South Vietnam, the weaker that country's own effort became, while the will of North Vietnam stiffened under heavy bombing. More tons of bombs fell on Vietnam than were dropped on all fronts during World War II. While thousands of American soldiers died and were wounded in battle, uncounted Vietnamese soldiers and villagers, men, women, and children, were killed and maimed from bombs and napalm, a chemical fire-weapon. A chemical defoliant, Agent Orange, destroyed forests and crops.

Still the North Vietnamese fought on. President Johnson swore he would never be the first American President to lose a war. His pride, and the pride of America, was at stake. He dreamed of vast American aid projects to rebuild Vietnam, once the Communists were forever defeated.

As the war escalated, the President worked longer and longer hours to the point where I felt he must keel over. He'd leave the Oval Office at one or two in the morning, taking with him a big armload of papers to work on upstairs. Then he expected his Situation Re-

ports brought to him in his bed between five and six
A.M.

The President wanted me and Mr. Harriston to bring
him his reports. We weren't supposed to be at work
until seven A.M., but we took turns being "early man"
so that one of us would always be there at five o'clock.
President Johnson wanted his seven or eight newspapers and the Situation Reports, and someone had to be
there to make sure he got them. The reports gave him
exact details on everything that had happened in Vietnam in the past twenty four hours: how many of our
men had been killed and wounded, whether the troops
had advanced or retreated, and what bombing raids
had been planned and completed.

When it was my turn, at five A.M. I'd go up to the
West Hall outside the President's bedroom and look
under the door. If there was a light showing then I'd
know he was up. I'd knock gently, and the President
would say softly, "Come in!" We didn't want to disturb
Mrs. Johnson, who was sleeping quietly on the right
side of the President's huge bed, which was ten or
twelve feet wide, with canopy and curtains all around.

President Johnson had a small light to read by on his
side of the bed. Next to it was a table piled high with
papers. When I'd come in, he'd be working away. If I
didn't see him in bed, I knew he was probably in the
bathroom. There was a desk there, too, for him to work
on.

One morning I didn't get to the White House until
five-thirty, and the usual mound of papers for the President weren't in the Usher's Office. I figured that one of
the Secret Service men must have taken the papers

upstairs, even though the President wanted Mr. Harriston or me to bring him his work.

Sure enough, a Secret Service man soon arrived at the Usher's Office complaining, "The President just threw me out of his bedroom! He said to me, 'What the hell are *you* doing up here?'"

I said, "Well, I guess old Maude had to kick you!" That was an old saying of my father's. It meant that despite warning he had to find out for himself that the President only wanted me and Mr. Harriston to bring up his reports. He learned his lesson and never went up there again.

One Saturday in February 1966, there was a terrible blizzard in Washington. It was snowing so hard I barely made it back home, the driving was so treacherous. I was on duty that Sunday, and I dreaded trying to get back to the White House through all that snow. But I knew that for President Johnson that snowy Sunday morning would be just like any other day. His Situation Reports would roll in and he expected me to bring them to him.

I got up at four and called the White House and asked them to send a car for me.

"Sorry, Bruce," I was told. "*Nothing* is moving this morning."

I had a big pair of gum boots, and I pushed my pants down inside them and dressed as warmly as I could.

It was still snowing hard when I left home. It was windy and the snowdrifts were blowing. I started to walk in the middle of the street, where the last car had gone through. I didn't see a single car, or a person. Nothing moved, not even when I got to 14th Street. The snow was deep and heavy—almost up to my knees. I walked down 14th Street, but there was no bus. I kept walking. After about three miles, a bus came by. By that time I was so overheated from all the slogging through the snow in heavy clothes, that when I got on the bus everything began to spin around and I went limp. An elderly man sitting next to me said, "My goodness, mister! You are having a heart attack!"

He pulled a little bottle from his pocket and said, "Put this on your tongue!"

It was nitroglycerine. I did as he said, and just the minute the little tablet disintegrated, I began to breathe. I rode on for a little. The man asked me where I was going, and I told him the White House. I began to feel a little better, but I was so tired that I couldn't have gotten off the bus and walked right then. I felt as though it would have killed me.

Five or six blocks farther on, the man gave me another tablet and I began to feel lots better. I sat up.

He looked me over and said, "Maybe you are all right. Have you ever had a heart attack."

"No!"

Just before he left, he gave me two more tablets to take before I got off the bus. By the time I got off the bus, my chest was hurting. I felt as if somebody had a rope around me, pulling it tight. But I made it from 14th and G Streets to the North Gate of the White House, taking my time, getting my breath as best I could. The snow there wasn't quite as deep and heavy for me to walk in.

The policeman at the gate walked in with me. We went straight to Dr. Young who put me on the table and gave me an electrocardiagram. He said, "I don't know how you missed a massive thrombosis. You strained your heart, but you've had no brain damage. You're going to be all right."

I had to stay home for three months after that—Mr. Harriston worked thirteen days out of fourteen until I returned.

When I was ready to return to work, President Johnson ordered a special parking place for me on East Executive Avenue, where his top aides from the Oval Office parked their cars, so I wouldn't have far to walk after I parked my car. I was told to take a rest anytime I felt I needed to. J. B. West provided me with my own dressing room on the mezzanine. For a full hour or more each day, I'd go there, pull my shoes off, and relax in a big, luxurious old reclining chair.

I was glad to be back at work. The President needed me more and more. Everything was going wrong for him—in Vietnam and on the home front. His standing with the voters sank to a new low in the public opinion polls. Every day President Johnson came back from the Oval Office either in a tearing rage, or feeling so discouraged that it worried us terribly.

Mr. Valenti observed that I was able to calm the President down when he got upset better than anyone else. I didn't do all that much. I'd just let him storm for a bit, then I'd say, "Now, Mr. President, could I get you some coffee? Would you like something?" And he'd quiet down and say, "Yes, Bruce. That's a good idea."

I've often thought about why President Johnson and I came to understand each other so well. In the beginning I'd actually thought I would rather quit than work for him.

One day he asked me, "Didn't you grow up on a

farm?" I told him, "Yes, I did." And he said, "So did I!" He asked if my father owned his own land, and I told him that he hadn't, but we had our own livestock and my father had his own barber shop in town.

He then talked about his father's hard times, and how his family had to leave their farm when he was small. None of the President's top aides had grown up poor in the rural South as he and I had. We shared a common beginning.

By the spring of 1967, four hundred thousand American soldiers were in Vietnam. Casualties were mounting and opposition to the war burst into flame. Many Americans decided, no matter what the consequences, it was time to get out. From small beginnings on the college campuses, grew a "peace movement" of great size. Martin Luther King, Jr. came out against the war at this time, and Senator Robert Kennedy decided he had to speak out forcefully. On May 2, he gave a ringing speech in the Senate Chamber that made President Lyndon B. Johnson his enemy.

Senator Kennedy asked the American people to feel responsible for the suffering of the Vietnamese people caused by American bombs and weapons. It was, he said, "not just a nation's responsibility, but yours and mine. It is we who live in abundance and send our young men out to die. It is our chemicals that scorch the children and our bombs that level the villages. We are all participants. . . . We are not in Vietnam to play the role of avenging angel pouring death and destruction on the roads and factories and homes of a guilty land. We are there to assure the self-determination of South Vietnam. . . ."

Senator Kennedy's speech helped to fuel the peace

movement. A great protest march on the Pentagon was planned for October 17, 1967. Unfortunately, the march on the Pentagon was not as unified and well-disciplined as the civil rights march of 1963. There was a small group of protestors bent on violence—a few hundred out of seventy to ninety thousand people. The leaders of the march on the Pentagon could not control this band of "crazies," who ran amuck, desecrating the American flag, shouting "Hey, hey, LBJ, how many kids have you killed today?"

Once again I stood at the Solarium window with a President. But this time, instead of the swelling chorus of "We Shall Overcome," we heard the ugly taunts and the wailing of police sirens. The window was closed against bitter-smelling tear gas. President Johnson was shaken. "Do you think I'm doing the right thing, Bruce?" he agonized.

I tried to reassure him, "Mr. President, I don't see how you could do any more. These people don't understand what you are trying to do. They shouldn't be allowed to carry on like this."

"No, no, Bruce," said the President. "They must have their say. This is a free country."

I felt very angry toward those demonstrators who acted violently. I carried with me my father's and mother's teaching to always stay within the law. If you don't like it, wait until it is changed; in the meantime, control your anger. I felt the demonstrators were misinformed. They thought the President wanted to prolong the war, and I knew he was desperate to end it, but on terms that would not spell defeat for the United States.

A few weeks later, Senator Eugene McCarthy announced his bid for the Democratic presidential nomination—one of the few times in U.S. history that a sitting President has been seriously challenged for renomination within his own party. At first, few took McCarthy seriously. But as thousands of young people, some not even old enough to vote, flocked to the senator's campaign to work for him at little or no pay, the President began to realize the threat was real.

On November 29, Robert McNamara resigned his post as Secretary of Defense and became head of the World Bank.

On January 30, 1968, the North Vietnamese forces came out of the jungle to strike South Vietnam with the "Tet Offensive"—a surprise attack on thirty South Vietnamese cities, including the capital, Saigon, where the U.S. Embassy came under attack.

After Tet, the Joint Chiefs of Staff asked that two hundred thousand more soldiers be sent to Vietnam, while Robert Kennedy, in Chicago on February 8, made his most passionate speech yet on Vietnam. He expressed his horror at the bombing and destruction, and at the corrupt Saigon government in South Vietnam. He urged that the North Vietnamese be given a place in any new government to come.

Senator Kennedy roused strong feelings with this speech—some felt him courageous, while others called him a traitor.

Soon after Tet, seven major newspapers came out for ending the war, and critics of the President spoke out on Capitol Hill, within the Democratic Party, the Cabinet, even inside the White House staff, and the President's own Senior Advisory Group.

\*      \*      \*

Above all else, the President dreaded that Robert Kennedy would enter the race for President against him. Lyndon Johnson had picked up the mantle of the slain hero, John F. Kennedy. Now to face a contest with Kennedy's own brother was the cruelest of prospects.

On March 12, in the New Hampshire primary, Senator Eugene McCarthy with his band of young volunteers, called the "Children's Crusade," pulled in a staggering 42 percent of the vote against the power of a sitting President. Four days later, Robert Kennedy declared himself a candidate for President.

Now the President opened himself up to me in a way he never had before. We were riding down from the second floor in the elevator.

"Bruce," he began, "do you think I've done a good job as President? Have I made any headway in civil rights? Do you think I've tried to stop the war?"

I said, "Mr. President, I don't think any President could have done better." Perhaps my words were shallow, but I believed in and admired the sincere way he went about things. Then the President said, "Stop this elevator!"

And we stood there, talking very low, after the elevator had landed on the ground floor. The President said, "You know, all of these blankety-blanks on the newspapers don't think I'm doing a good job. It's not fair! I didn't make that war over there. That was already going on when I became President." He leaned down his head and whispered hoarsely into my ear, "You know what I'm going to do, Bruce? I'm going to give them this job! I am *not* going to run again!" Then he narrowed his eyes and warned me, "Listen, if I hear this anywhere, I will know where it is coming from. And I better *not* hear it!"

I believe that no one else knew of the President's decision not to run again, except for the First Family and Mr. Valenti.

On March 31, 1968, the President went on nationwide TV. He announced a pause in the bombing, and that no more troops would be sent to Vietnam.

He said, "I am taking the first step to de-escalate the conflict." He stopped to take a quick look at Lady Bird, then he continued, "There is division in the American house now. . . . With America's sons in the fields far away, with America's future under challenge right here at home. . . . I do not believe that I should devote an hour or a day of my time to any personal partisan causes. . . . Accordingly I shall not seek, and will not accept, the nomination of my party for another term as your President."

A few days later, the North Vietnamese agreed to peace talks in Paris.

The President was praised everywhere for his unselfish act. His popularity in the polls shot from 36 percent to 49 percent.

Only four days after President Johnson's announcement, Martin Luther King, Jr. was murdered in Memphis, Tennessee, by an escaped convict, James Earl Ray, a forty-year-old white man. In cities all over the United States, black ghettos erupted in grief and rage. Washington, D.C., was hard hit. The White House called me at home to say, "Don't come to work today, Bruce. It's not safe to be out on the streets."

I missed one day's work and the next day I drove to

the White House, avoiding lower 14th Street, the most dangerous area. National Guard troops, helmeted and carrying rifles with fixed bayonets, were everywhere. Never did I expect to see that in the city where I lived, the nation's capital. For days the smoke drifted over the city—you could smell it everywhere, including at the White House.

The day of Martin Luther King, Jr.'s death, Robert Kennedy was campaigning for the presidency, scheduled to speak that night in heart of the Indianapolis ghetto. The police chief told him not to go to the meeting but he brushed the warning aside. His police escort left him. They could not guarantee his safety and they feared for themselves. Senator Kennedy climbed on a flatbed truck. A TV newsman described him "up there, hunched in his black overcoat, his face gaunt and full of anguish." The crowd gathered there had not yet heard the news.

Robert Kennedy said, "I have bad news for you, for all of our fellow citizens, and people who love peace all over the world, and that is that Martin Luther King was shot and killed tonight." A terrible shudder ran through the crowd. He went on, "Martin Luther King dedicated his life to love and to justice for his fellow human beings, and he died because of that effort. . . . For those of you who are black and are tempted to be filled with hatred and distrust at the injustice of such an act, against all white people, I can only say that I feel in my own heart the same kind of feeling. I had a member of my family killed, but he was killed by a white man. But we have to make an effort to understand, to go beyond these rather difficult times. . . .

"The vast majority of white people and the vast ma-

jority of black people in this country want to live together, want to improve the quality of our life, and
want justice for all human beings. . . .

"Let us dedicate ourselves to what the Greeks wrote
so many years ago, to tame the savageness of man and
to make gentle the life of this world. . . ."

No harm came to Robert F. Kennedy that night in
the black ghetto of Indianapolis. The campaign between Eugene McCarthy and Robert Kennedy grew
bitter; then Vice-President Hubert Humphrey's bid
made it a three-way race. Kennedy won the primary in
Nebraska, but in Oregon he lost to McCarthy—the first
time the magic name of Kennedy had lost a political
contest. Next came California, a crucial primary.

Robert Kennedy had started his campaign late, with
no national organization, no convention delegates, no
campaign staff. So he went straight to the people, to
move them by the power and passion of his speeches.
He stirred deep feelings in many who listened to him
—feelings of intense love and feelings of bitter hatred.
In California, Kennedy was mobbed by a friendly
crowd in Watts and spat upon by students at San Fran-
cisco State College. He allowed friendly crowds to maul
him, saying, "Well, so many people hate me that I've
got to give the people who love me a chance to get at
me."

He refused protection, saying, "I'm not afraid of anybody. If things happen, they're going to happen." And
he said, "If there is somebody out there who wants to
get me, well, doing anything in public life today is Russian roulette."

At last the California results came in: Kennedy got

more votes than Humphrey and McCarthy combined. In his victory speech at the Hotel Ambassador in Los Angeles, Robert Kennedy spoke of the "divisions . . . between blacks and whites, between the poor and more affluent, between age groups or on the war in Vietnam." He went on, "We can start to work together. . . . We are a great country, an unselfish country, a compassionate country."

With the cheers of the victory celebration ringing in his ears, Robert Kennedy left the hotel ballroom to go to a press conference. He took a shortcut through the kitchen and was gunned down in a narrow hallway by a young Jordanian, Sirhan Bishara Sirhan.

I was in the White House that evening when the news of Robert Kennedy's death came in. I kept saying to myself, I knew this was going to happen, I knew it. I always felt about Robert Kennedy the same as I did about all the Presidents. When I saw them board Air Force helicopters on the South Lawn, I worried that I might never see them again alive. But I felt that Robert Kennedy was in even more danger than the others. He was just too controversial for his own good. He was the dynamic force behind all the civil rights enforcement of the Kennedy administration. He stuck his neck out and exercised the kind of force that was detrimental to himself. People called him a fanatic.

Robert Kennedy wanted a better life not only for blacks but for any underdogs. He was for the poor, regardless. The Kennedy brothers, John and Robert and Ted, grew up rich all their lives, yet they understood what it is like to be poor. When they were still in school, they'd go down to the Boston shipyards and talk to working people. They learned what the poor man was fighting for, what he had to have.

President Johnson grew up poor and he cared about poor people too. He was unlike many other politicians whose attitude is "I made it, why can't you? You should pull yourself up by your bootstraps." They don't seem to understand that they had bootstraps to pull on and a lot of poor people don't.

Even though they had split apart over Vietnam, President Johnson was deeply saddened by Robert Kennedy's death. I heard him say how "senseless" it seemed to him.

The Democratic Convention, in August, was a disaster. Despite Senator McCarthy's pleas to stay away from Chicago, thousands of young "peaceniks" came to demonstrate. Some threw rocks and yelled obscenities. There were pitched battles between demonstrators and angry policemen who clubbed not only violent demonstrators but also peaceful ones and innocent bystanders and newsmen as well. Inside Convention Hall, the delegates wrangled violently over the Vietnam plank for the Party Platform. When it was all over, the Democratic Party was splintered and its nominee, Hubert Humphrey, had a poor chance to win against Richard Nixon in November.

In the climate of despair over the assassinations, frustration over the war and turmoil at home, President Johnson could not move ahead with his Great Society. He'd hoped the Paris peace talks might end the war, but in October they bogged down. In November, Richard Nixon defeated Hubert Humphrey and George Wallace in the presidential election.

\* \* \*

On the afternoon of December 17, 1968, just before Lyndon Johnson left the White House, the President stopped at the Usher's Office and asked me what time I went off duty. I told him six o'clock.

"You're going with me to a reception tonight. Come to my office at seven o'clock," he ordered. Then, without a word of explanation, he left for the Oval Office.

I was startled and chagrined that, wherever the President was taking me, I'd have to wear the same old suit I'd put on that morning. But, promptly at seven o'clock, I went to the Oval Office. There the President ushered me out the door and into his limousine.

At the Sheraton Carlton Hotel, in downtown Washington, a group of high black officials, including Supreme Court Justice Thurgood Marshall, were waiting to honor President Johnson for appointing many black people to important government jobs. In the audience, I saw my daughter Elaine and her husband William Pryor, a judge of Superior Court. They'd had no idea I would be there.

The President steered me through the crowded ballroom up to the dais where the dignitaries waited. He went to the microphone and I stood next to him while he spoke:

"I came over tonight with one of my dear friends. His name is Preston Bruce. He was born a year after I was born. He has been in the White House faithfully serving many, many Presidents. Outside of my wife and family, who give me great comfort in moments of need, this great American gentleman, Preston Bruce, has kept me going."

As I listened to President Johnson, I wished my father could have been by my side.

After the Johnsons went back to Texas, they planned a dedication ceremony for the Lyndon B. Johnson Library. I got a special invitation to travel to Austin, Texas, with the Texas congressional delegation.

At the dedication I sat with Congressman Jack Brooks and former Secretary of State Dean Rusk. From upstairs, Lyndon Johnson called down for me. He introduced me to his Texas friends and told them about my career.

In August, 1972, I received a letter from the LBJ Ranch in Texas. It read:

Dear Preston,

It brightened my birthday to hear from you again. It stirred some White House memories.

Thank you for making me feel missed and remembered.

Sincerely,
(signed) Lyndon B. Johnson

At the bottom of the letter are these words, written in ink in the President's own handwriting:

I love you and yours. L.

# Chapter 5

# THE NIXONS

ONLY three or four days after the election, in November 1968, strange things began to happen at the White House. Lyndon Johnson was still the President. He and his family wouldn't leave until the following January when Richard Nixon was inaugurated as President.

Several times I saw a new name on the visitor's list in the Usher's Office: John D. Ehrlichman. He had appointments with Chief Usher J. B. West and with Mrs. Kaltman, the housekeeper. As Mr. West, Mr. John Ficklen, the maitre d', and Mrs. Kaltman took time to show Mr. Ehrlichman all over the White House, I heard this man asking minute questions about the way things were run. No detail seemed too small to escape his curiosity.

All this made me very uneasy. Never before in my

141

experience, had a political aide to a newly elected President come snooping into every part of the White House before the current President had left the mansion. We on the household staff already knew how to make the first families safe and comfortable—that was *our* job. What did this man plan to do?

Those visits continued. Every time I turned around, there was John Ehrlichman, his big shoulders hunched forward, pushing his way into the Usher's Office or elsewhere in the White House. At the same time, I was hearing ominous reports about another aide to President-elect Richard Nixon—Bob Haldeman—whom I'd not yet seen. Keep away from this man, I was told, because he's a tough customer, a hatchet man. That was a bad thing to hear, not knowing whose head a hatchet man can reach out and cut off.

For fifteen years I'd studied powerful presidential aides: men like Governor Sherman Adams, for President Eisenhower, Ted Sorenson and Ken O'Donnell for President Kennedy, and Jack Valenti and Marvin Watson for President Johnson. I'd marveled at the true devotion all the men had had to their Presidents. My colleagues and I had instinctively trusted these men completely.

I felt exactly the opposite toward John D. Ehrlichman and Bob Haldeman.

But my spirits rose as I stood at the South Entrance on January 20, 1969, and welcomed President Nixon and his family to their new home. The next morning, President and Mrs. Nixon and their daughters Tricia and Julie started learning the names of all eighty of us on the household staff—every houseman, maid, butler,

Secret Service man, carpenter, electrician—all the people who served them. This pleased us all—it was something new.

A few days later, the Nixons held a state dinner. At 7:00 P.M., I was standing at the Usher's Office waiting for my escort cards to be delivered from the Social Office. Suddenly, a strange man with a large camera slung around his neck started to bound up the Grand Staircase toward the family quarters on the second floor. He was athletic, suntanned, wiry, and tall, with a big chin and a sandy crewcut. I reached out and grabbed him, fast.

"Just a minute, please," I said. "I don't believe I know you!"

The man grinned, but his bright blue eyes were cold and hard.

"I'm Bob Haldeman," he said.

"I'm sorry, Mr. Haldeman," I apologized. "I didn't recognize you."

About a week later, President Nixon made a point to introduce me to both Mr. Haldeman and Mr. Ehrlichman. Both men greeted me cordially at that time. But never, ever again over the six years that Mr. Nixon was in office, did either of these two gentlemen acknowledge me in any way. They chose to ignore me. Hundreds of times they'd need the elevator. Each time they'd say, curtly, "Take me to the second floor," without so much as a please or thank you. They looked right through me as if I were invisible. Other than these terse instructions, they never spoke a single word to me.

The President always went out of his way to greet and talk with me—football was a favorite subject between us. Even though these conversations often took place in front of Mr. Haldeman and Mr. Ehrlichman, they'd stand by, stony-faced, fixing their eyes on some distant point across the room. They acted the same way toward all the rest of the household staff. They were loners.

A memo went out from Mr. Haldeman's office to everyone saying that anybody asking the President or any member of his family for an autographed picture or a favor would be fired on the spot—no matter how long he or she had worked at the White House. We all felt this was a cheap little shot. We knew better than to approach the President with such requests and no one had ever done such a thing, not in my time there. So why send out a memorandum to that effect? I believe the purpose was to make us feel small, to keep everybody down as low as possible. No one was supposed to peep his head up or to assume to have friendly contact with the President.

There was a steady stream of memos like that telling us what to do. We had years of experience to guide us and, as far as any of us knew, never before had political aides to a President interfered this way with the household staff of the White House.

In Europe, Mr. Haldeman had seen royal police forces dressed in elaborate, pretentious uniforms. For our White House policemen, he ordered new uniforms, thick with gold braid and tassels, which they hated. For a whole year they wore costumes that were ridiculed in the newspapers.

At state dinners, every previous president had been glad to have us stand in the hall outside the State Dining Room after dinner was cleared away to hear the toasts between the President and the visiting dignitaries. Mr. Haldeman issued a brusque memo saying *nobody* was allowed in the hall during state dinners—not even Secret Service men.

Mr. Haldeman's office tried to take away my parking space—but backed down on that when my doctor insisted I needed it. They did, however, succeed in exchanging my comfortable dressing room for a tiny, dark cubicle. These were small things, clearly calculated to make us miserable. It caused me to worry about the President. What would happen to *him* with men like these in the driver's seat? However, there was nothing to do but push these things to the back of my mind and polish new skills.

It was during the Nixon years that people in the State Department began to ask me for help on protocol. They knew I was able to handle foreign diplomats who came to the White House and put them at ease whether or not they spoke English.

I was given a loose-leaf notebook with a page for every country represented here in the United States. The page would show a picture of the country's ambassador, with information about him and his nation. When that ambassador left Washington, I discarded his page and the State Department gave me a new one for his replacement. I was the only person on our staff to have one of these notebooks, which I studied and found useful in talking to the diplomats.

One of the trickiest situations I had to handle was the Presentation of Credentials. That's when a new ambassador comes to the White House to pay his formal respects to the President, according to international rules of protocol. The President's time is so valuable, he can give each ambassador only about seven minutes with two minutes allowed between each one.

It would be easy if just one ambassador came at a time, but we sometimes had as many as seven at once. The problem is that every ambassador wants to feel that he's the only one coming to present his credentials to the President. He wants to believe that it is his nation that is most important to the President that day. So he mustn't see any of the other ambassadors. He mustn't even know they're in the White House. I had to receive each one, find a comfortable place for him to wait, and try to figure out a way to shift him in and out of the Diplomatic Reception Room so he'd never catch a glimpse of another ambassador. If any one were ever five minutes late, it was a disaster. Rex Scouten, the new Chief Usher, was happy when I took over this job.

Each country has a different style—that was always interesting to me. And foreign diplomats know the complicated laws of protocol very well, much better than most people do here in America. You have to handle them accordingly, because they're quick to take offense.

For instance, the diplomats rank each other by how long they've served in a certain post. The dean of the Diplomatic Corps in a certain city is the ambassador who's been there the longest. He's a very important person no matter how small the country he represents may be.

Here in Washington, the dean was Ambassador Sevilla-Secasa of Nicaragua, a man I learned to know and like.

He was fond of me, too, which turned out to be lucky. One evening, President Nixon was having a big reception for the Diplomatic Corps. A new policeman was on duty that night and he asked each diplomat to show his identification as he drove up to the gate.

When this happened to Ambassador Sevilla-Secasa, he got furious. *Everybody* was supposed to know who he was! He berated the policeman, then he told his chauffeur to turn the car around and take him back home to the Nicaraguan Embassy. When he got there, he phoned someone in the State Department and threatened to create a big explosion, to file a formal diplomatic protest. Since he'd been insulted at the White House, he said, that automatically meant that his government had also been insulted.

The State Department called the Usher's Office, and poor Mr. Scouten was aghast.

"Bruce, we've got a problem," he told me. "The State Department people have talked Ambassador Sevilla-Secasa into coming back to the White House tonight, but I hate to think what he'll do when he gets here."

"May I go out to meet him?" I asked.

"By all means," said Mr. Scouten, "and good luck!"

I waited outside, at the North Entrance, for the Nicaraguan limousine. The minute it rolled up, I caught the door handle, opened it, and reached inside for the Ambassador's hand.

"My friend!" the Ambassador cried, "Let me tell you about this terrible insult I have suffered!"

"Oh I know, I know, Mr. Ambassador, we're heartbroken you've had this awful experience," I said. I told him about the new policeman.

"I must write to the State Department!" he insisted.

I put my arm around his shoulder and I quieted him down. Mr. Scouten came out and made a fuss over him and took him into the reception. The President had been briefed and came over especially to greet the Ambassador, and his fellow diplomats made a point to pay their respects.

It all blew over, but it was a very chilly situation for a while.

Celebrities from the entertainment world often visited the White House. Bob Hope was my favorite. He visited a lot, and one time I remember especially.

It was during a state visit. Bob Hope and his wife, Dolores, arrived about two in the afternoon, and I took them upstairs to the Queen's Room.

As usual, Bob Hope kidded me. He said, "Bruce, you're so starched and ironed, you ought to be the President."

He went on to ask questions about my job and how the White House worked. He was interested in the way we were able to handle so many different types of functions.

President Nixon liked the Hopes so well, he wanted their visits to be special. While all of us on the staff were downstairs getting ready for the state dinner, the President went into the Queen's Sitting Room and put a match to the carefully laid logs in the fireplace. However, it was the only fireplace that didn't work!

Smoke poured out across the hall and into the dressing room where Mrs. Hope's clothes had been unpacked and laid out by the maids. What a mess!

We closed off the smoky room and opened up all the windows, and with the help of two big fans we got the smoke out. But just when everything calmed down, Bob Hope came running out of the bedroom in a panic.

"My script! I can't find it!" he cried. "I've got to memorize my routine for the show tonight!"

He was going to entertain the guests in the East Room after the state dinner. I helped him search his briefcase and his suitcase but the script was nowhere to be seen. He'd left it behind. He got on the phone to California and had someone dictate to him. He had to write down his whole act longhand. By this time it was getting late.

Mr. Hope said, "Bruce, I can't go down to dinner tonight. I'll have to stay up here and memorize my routine."

I told Mr. Scouten that since the butlers were busy with the state dinner, after I finished receiving the guests, I'd serve Mr. Hope's dinner. I brought the dinner tray to the Lincoln Sitting Room where Mr. Hope was working. As I was about to leave, he said, "Bruce are you busy? Do you have to run off?"

I sat in a tall chair by the desk, and he sat in the President's big chair and we talked. I told him, "You've always been an idol of mine. I don't believe I've missed one of your shows on TV!"

That was true and he liked to hear it.

I said, "I've watched you grow into maturity."

"What! Do you mean I'm an old man?" he protested.

"Oh no!" I said. "You'll never grow old!"

I told him I'd give anything if I could appear before big audiences and stay as calm as he did. But he said, "No! Every time I go on stage, I'm scared stiff, nervous as a cat. I get over it once I warm up."

I didn't believe him.

"Yes, Bruce, it's *true*," he said. "You never know what's going to happen when you walk out there."

That surprised me. I'd never have thought an experienced professional like Bob Hope would get stage fright.

President Nixon started something new at the White House—Sunday services in the East Room. The Secret Service thought this was a marvelous idea—the President staying in the White House instead of going outside where something could happen to him. I felt the same way. I worked every one of the services, even when it was on one of my days off.

At every Sunday service we were crowded—always two hundred and fifty to three hundred people. I greeted everyone and handed out the special programs, which the President would autograph for the choir and the guest minister.

Reverend Billy Graham preached at many of the Sunday services, and I admired him. If he didn't see me, he'd ask for me. He was a close friend of the President's and often stayed overnight at the White House.

President Nixon planned every detail of those services himself, and afterward he'd stand out in the hall and visit with his guests. He was at his best at those times. It was good to see him so relaxed and happy.

All the staff was invited to those services and that's how I came to know many of the President's top aides from the Oval Office.

Former Marine Corps Captain Charles Colson was one of the senior aides. He never missed a Sunday service. He was a stocky, enthusiastic man. He liked to wear polka dot ties. He was pleasant to me and I liked him.

A favorite of mine was the President's Press Secretary, Ron Ziegler. He was clean cut and energetic. I'd come over to his office and tie his white tie for him when we had a formal affair because he just couldn't get the hang of it. He was very warm and responsive to me, and Steve Bull was too. Those two had no ax to grind, they were just looking after the President, trying to make good in their jobs.

I came to know the President's Attorney General, John Mitchell, who later became campaign manager at the Committee to Reelect the President (CRP). He'd been President Nixon's law partner and close friend in New York, so he had a direct pipeline to the President —he didn't have to go through Haldeman or Ehrlichman like everyone else. John Mitchell was an older man, stooped and balding, slow in his movements. He had no background or experience in politics. He was always very polite to me, yet so grave and silent. He acted worried and preoccupied. I felt there must be deep things on his mind.

Another Nixon aide was John Dean, a young lawyer who'd been under Mitchell in the Justice Department before he came to the White House. Tall and bespectacled, with his wide forehead and large eyes, he looked like a scholarly young university professor. His mind, like John Mitchell's, often seemed far away. I saw John Dean only a few times, but I paid careful attention to him because he was the President's personal counsel, and I knew he was very close to Haldeman and Ehrlichman as well. But John Dean seemed to me and to others to be much less ruthless and hardboiled than Bob Haldeman and John Erlichman. We wondered how he could survive with them.

Tensions at the Nixon White House mounted noticeably in 1971. Senator George McGovern announced for the Democratic nomination for president in January, unusually early, since the election was twenty-one months away. His main issue was peace. He bitterly criticized President Nixon because the war in Vietnam still dragged on.

A few months later, in June, the Pentagon Papers burst into the news. Daniel Ellsberg, a combat veteran of Vietnam, employed by the Rand Corporation with top Pentagon security clearance, secretly photocopied major Pentagon files relating to the war in Vietnam and gave them to the newspapers. Despite strenuous efforts by the Justice Department, the Supreme Court refused to prevent the newspapers from publishing. These files, known as the Pentagon Papers, exposed mistakes that the United States had made in Vietnam. For the first time Americans learned that many military men within the Pentagon had been opposed to the war and our conduct of it.

Though the Pentagon Papers mainly showed mistakes in the Kennedy and Johnson years, the effect on the Nixon people was electric. They became obsessed with security, with the need to plug "leaks." As these "leaks" spread from real defense and foreign relations secrets to political operations, the Nixon people began to move against their possible "enemies" in ways no one dreamed of before.

All of us on the White House staff could tell that many

of the Nixon people, most of all Haldeman and Ehrlichman, were angry and felt under attack. We didn't know
exactly what they were doing—we didn't want to
know. It was bound to be something we wouldn't like.

For me, the worst part was the deception practiced
by Ehrlichman and Haldeman. They acted one way in
front of the President and another behind his back. I
watched the way Haldeman and Ehrlichman maneuv-
ered and what they were trying to do for themselves.
There were certain moves they made that I would pick
up on, that the President didn't see. They didn't bother
about my presence; they didn't care enough about me
to hide what they felt or said. It was obvious these men
were more interested in their own power and objec-
tives than in the President's future. They were feather-
ing their own nests, rather than helping the President
keep his nest together.

I felt a deep foreboding. I told my friends that I
feared those men might double-cross everybody, even
including the President. I feared the worst.

Watergate—and the downfall of President Richard
M. Nixon—broke out into the open on Saturday, June
17, 1972, one year after the release of the Pentagon
Papers. The President's reelection campaign was in full
swing and he was considered a shoo-in.

At first I thought it didn't sound like much. At two
o'clock on that Saturday morning, five men broke into
the headquarters of the Democratic National Committee in the Watergate Hotel and Office Building com-
plex, on the Potomac River a couple of miles from the
White House. An alert security guard, a young black

man named Frank Wills, noticed the stairwell doors to the sixth floor had been taped and then retaped. He called the police.

Instead of the usual squad car with two uniformed policemen, the police sent their plain clothes "mod squad" in an unmarked car. So the burglars' lookout man stationed across Virginia Avenue at a window of the Howard Johnson Motel saw nothing unusual. The "mod squad" caught the burglars in the act. Within a few days, news stories told of address books and other evidence that linked the burglars to both the White House and the Committee to Reelect the President.

The President had been at his vacation home in Key Biscayne, Florida. He flew back to Washington. We had not expected him at the White House until later in the week. I waited for the President that afternoon on the South Portico. As the helicopter roared overhead, then dropped down on the White House lawn, I asked myself, what will all this mean for President Nixon's administration?

He walked across the grass and Bob Haldeman went forward to meet him. They stopped and spoke together, heads bowed. While they were talking, I took Mrs. Nixon and Julie upstairs, noticing that Mrs. Nixon was far from her usual self—she seemed disturbed and unhappy.

I went back to get the President. He forced a smile when he saw me, but his mood was grim. He and Mr. Haldeman swept past other aides who were waiting for him in the lobby.

"Take us right up to the second floor, please, Bruce," he said. Normally he would have gone to the Oval Office.

Inside the elevator I saw President Nixon turn and face Bob Haldeman. His voice had a hard edge I'd never heard before, along with a definite note of surprise.

"Bob," he said, "what in the world did they expect to find over there?"

Mr. Haldeman shook his head emphatically and I heard him say, "Mr. President, *no one* in the White House had anything to do with *that.*" As it turned out, that was a lie. But his manner was quite convincing. He sounded sympathetic and sincere.

The President seemed relieved.

"Okay then. I want you to find out *immediately* exactly what went on down there and get back to me," he ordered. "I've got to go to the American people and explain it."

"Yes sir, yes sir. I'll get right on it," said Bob Haldeman.

He didn't get out of the elevator with the President as he always did, but went back down with me, showing the President he meant to carry out his orders pronto.

As I rode down to the first floor side by side with Mr. Haldeman, I had a sick feeling in the pit of my stomach. I didn't believe one word this man had said to the President.

During the next eight months, the FBI, the Justice Department, and a committee of the U.S. Senate under Senator Sam Ervin of North Carolina, along with the press, all investigated Watergate.

At the Ervin committee hearings in July 1973, Alexander Butterfield, a security man at the White House whom I knew and liked, revealed under oath that the Oval Office was "bugged" with sophisticated, voice-activated wiring. President Nixon recorded every conversation that took place in his office. The tapes of these conversations later became crucial evidence of wrongdoing.

All in all, the revelations were shocking—of a massive cover-up of Watergate, of hush money to the burglars, of illegal political dirty tricks, millions in illegal campaign contributions, and much more. John Dean was a key witness to the crimes committed by Haldeman, Ehrlichman, Mitchell, and others as well as himself. Dean's testimony implicated the President as well.

On the morning of April 30, 1973, Congressman John Moss of California urged the leaders of the House of Representatives to open a formal inquiry into the possible impeachment of the President. Under the Constitution, the House may vote to impeach—remove from office—a sitting President for "high crimes and misdemeanors," and the Senate then sits as the Court of Impeachment with the Chief Justice presiding.

Later that same day, the White House announced that John Dean had been fired, while Haldeman, Ehrlichman, and Richard Kleindienst, the new Attorney General, were allowed to resign. That night, I watched the President on television. His voice was hollow. Gone was the confident ring he usually had. I never heard it again.

That night the President said, to the American people:

"I want to talk to you again from my heart. . . . There had been an effort to conceal the facts both from the public, from you, and from me. . . . I wanted to be fair. . . . Today, in one of the most difficult decisions of my

Presidency, I accepted the resignations of two of my closest associates . . . Bob Haldeman and John Ehrlichman—two of the finest public servants it has been my privilege to know. . . . There can be no whitewash at the White House. . . . I love America. . . ."

The next day, May 1, I saw FBI men standing guard over the empty offices of Haldeman and Ehrlichman. I felt strange. There was a vacuum. The co-pilots were gone and the pilot was unsteady and no longer the strong man I once knew.

General Alexander Haig was appointed Chief of Staff to replace Haldeman, and that was a Godsend to us all. He was older, a settled man with good judgment, and we trusted him..

For more than a year, President Nixon held onto the White House, but it was downhill all the way.

I felt sorriest of all for Mrs. Nixon and the girls. Julie would come to me in tears, "Oh, Mr. Bruce," she'd cry. "How can they say such awful things about my father?"

"Never mind," I'd tell her. "Ignore all that. You know politics. It'll all come out right in the end."

But it didn't.

Mrs. Nixon kept on meeting her groups of White House visitors. She'd always been so outgoing and faithful in her duties—she did her job *well*. Once she shook 2,700 hands in a day and came out with her hands blistered. But now she was nervous and scared. As I brought her downstairs in the elevator, her voice would quaver as she asked me, "Bruce, do you think these people will be friendly?"

"They seem *very* friendly, Mrs. Nixon," I'd try to reassure her.

It broke my heart to see her go through the trauma of wondering how each group would treat her. She was a brave person to put herself through that again and again, when she could have refused. She was First Lady to the end.

Only rarely did anyone speak rudely to Mrs. Nixon, but now she dreaded exposing herself to anyone she didn't know. Through it all, no matter how fearful she was, never have I seen her when she didn't smile. She was a dear person, kind and thoughtful. How I wish she could have left the White House the proud way she came in.

By the spring of 1974, I knew there was no way the President could hold onto his office. By now I wanted him to go. It was very upsetting to me to see the President and Mrs. Nixon ground down day by day until they weren't themselves any more.

By then you couldn't feel natural with them—they were in such disgrace. It was painful and embarrassing for all of us to see a President and his family reduced to such a state.

On July 27, 29, and 30, 1974, the House of Representatives Judiciary Committee passed three separate articles of impeachment, charging the President with obstructing justice, with abuse of power, and with defying subpoenas for evidence.

On August 5, NBC said that 62 percent of the American people favored impeachment. On that same day, the President, under a court order, gave to the press transcripts of the Oval Office tapes of June 23, 1972, six days after the Watergate break-in. On the tapes, the President and Bob Haldeman discussed together ways to use the CIA to stop the FBI investigation of Watergate and what lay behind it.

In a statement released with the tape transcripts, the President admitted that parts of the tapes "are at variance with certain of my previous statements."

These tapes of June 23, 1972, were the "smoking gun" that exploded the last remnants of President Nixon's dwindling support on Capitol Hill.

On August 7, three key Republicans, Senators Scott and Goldwater plus the House Minority Leader, Congressman Rhodes, came to the Oval Office. They told the President, "The situation is very gloomy on Capitol Hill." President Nixon needed thirty-four Senate votes to stop impeachment; he could count on no more than fifteen.

Richard Nixon was a fighter. He hated more than anything to give up his office. But the longer he stayed, the more he risked not only impeachment but criminal prosecution. We hoped that if he would resign, for the good of the country, he'd be spared going to jail.

On August 8, at 12:23 P.M., Ron Ziegler came on the radio. His voice shook as he said:

"Tonight at nine o'clock Eastern Daylight Time, the President of the United States will address the nation on radio and television from his Oval Office."

On television that night, President Nixon sat at his desk with an American flag in his lapel. He looked drawn and ill. He said, "I have never been a quitter. To leave office before my term is completed is abhorrent to every instinct in my body. . . ." But, he said, to fight on "would almost totally absorb the time and attention of both the President and the Congress in a period when our entire focus should be on the great issues of peace abroad and prosperity without inflation at home."

Then the President said, "Therefore, I shall resign the Presidency effective at noon tomorrow."

The transfer of power was shockingly abrupt, yet orderly as it had been after the assassination of President Kennedy. We packed up the President and First Lady, Tricia and her husband Edward Cox, so that they could leave the White House in less than twenty-four hours. Julie and her husband, David Eisenhower, stayed behind with the sad task of removing the last of the family things out of the White House.

The next morning was one of the saddest days of my life. At about ten o'clock, the President left the Oval Office and walked over to meet me at the elevator. He looked terribly upset.

The doors closed, the elevator started, and for the first time, I saw Richard Nixon cry. He and I held onto one another. I, too, wept, as I had with Mrs. Kennedy and Robert.

I said, "Mr. President, this is a time in my life that I wish had never happened."

The President said to me, "I have in you a true friend."

I brought the whole Nixon family downstairs for the last time. They got off the elevator and we stood all together in the hallway. Tricia hugged me, the first time she'd ever done so. Her husband, Ed Cox, said, "Mr. Bruce, you have been an inspiration to this family."

Mrs. Nixon put her arms around me and so did Julie,

and David and the President. They thanked me for all I'd done for them. Then the Nixon family went to face all the White House staff waiting in the East Room for a final farewell. As they walked in, the Marine Band played "Hail to the Chief."

I'll always remember Richard Nixon saying, "This house has a great heart, and that heart comes from those who serve."

Then he broke down completely and sobbed, speaking of his mother and his sad childhood. I was heartbroken for Mrs. Nixon and the girls, having to stand up there with him on that stage, the whole family feeling the disgrace. Those people were living, and yet they were dead. It was just that simple.

As I watched the Nixons walk down the long red carpet to the helicopter, I was filled with emotion. This was a part of history that had never happened before —our first President to resign in office—and here I was, mixed right into the heart of it, seeing the last bit trickle out.

# Chapter 6

## THE FORDS

GERALD Ford was sworn in as President at 12:03 P.M. August 10, 1974, by Chief Justice Warren Burger. The new President said, ". . . Our long national nightmare is over. Our Constitution works. Our great republic is a government of laws and not of men."

Gerald R. Ford was one of the most cheerful, the most likable human beings I have yet to know. No one could get more tough and serious with his aides—he had a firm, confident sense of his authority—yet he was open-minded. He would listen, attentively, to whatever someone would tell him. He was so kind, so nice, it just didn't seem real. But, having known him for many years, I knew there was no put-on. From the first time

I met him until the last time we saw each other, he never changed.

President Ford resisted being spoiled. When he moved into the White House, he wanted to keep on making his own breakfast the way he had for years— English muffins, marmalade, and coffee. The butlers didn't like that, but at first they humored him. They'd come into the family kitchen and set it all up for him so he could go from there. But before too long, he gave way to their wishes and allowed them to serve him.

Every other President I knew had his own bedroom. But President Ford moved into the First Lady's bedroom and sent every stick of furniture from his room into storage. He turned his bedroom into an exercise room with his bike, mats, weights, and trophies displayed. I got a kick out of seeing him work out there every morning—he was a fantastic physical specimen with the movements of a young man. Anybody who tried to tangle with him would get a big surprise.

The Ford family was very close. The President allowed Mrs. Betty Ford to voice her own opinions openly to the press even if he disagreed—she came out for the Equal Rights Amendment for women though her husband, the President, opposed it. With his children, President Ford was strict but positive. He'd always listen to what they had to say. The boys told their father they had tried marijuana and when the press asked President Ford about it, he answered honestly.

The two Ford children who lived in the White House —Steve and Susan—were hard to spoil too. I'd see Susan refuse to let the Secret Service men carry her books, and I'd watch her blue-jean clad brother fixing his motorcycle in the White House driveway, while the Secret Service men, in their business suits, stood by and looked on.

Mrs. Ford and Susan were so tender it reminded me of my own wife and daughter. They were inseparable, and they were honest with each other.

Altogether, taking care of the Ford family was smooth sailing. But unfortunately, they hired young staff people who were inexperienced, and that made trouble for us old-timers at the White House. These newcomers didn't come and ask us how things should be done, as had Miss Tuckerman and Miss Baldridge on Mrs. Kennedy's staff. Mrs. Elizabeth Carpenter and Mrs. Bess Ahell were Mrs. Johnson's press and social secretaries. They were very efficient and wonderful to work with.

I remember the first time the President and the First Lady greeted a visiting head of state. That arrival ceremony must be planned down to the second, so that the letter-perfect arrangements will protect the dignity of both countries.

I looked for the flowers that the First Lady always presents to the wife of the visiting head of state. One of the new staff people was holding them. I didn't say anything because it was their ball game. I knew they were going to do something different and I wondered how it would turn out.

I stood in the Diplomatic Reception Room by the door, waiting for the military aide to give the President his cue to move out toward the cameras.

When an arriving head of state comes through the Southwest Gate, there is perhaps twenty seconds to get the President outside to meet him. Of course, the President mustn't be seen outside waiting for *anyone;* neither can he keep his honored guest waiting. The two heads of state must move simultaneously toward one another and connect. If either man appeared to overshadow or to defer to the other, it would make one country seem more or less important than the other, and that can't happen—the two nations must look equal.

The military aide got the message from the policeman at the Gate and he passed the cue on to the President. The President and the First Lady walked out the door . . . it was then I saw that the First Lady was carrying the flowers. It was terrible. But the cameras were blazing and it was too late to do anything about it.

A First Lady *never* walks out against the cameras carrying anything. She must move freely. After the two couples shake hands, someone waiting behind the scene gives the First Lady the flowers on cue, and she immediately presents them to her guest. The person who holds the flowers for the First Lady darts out of the way to be sure not to get into the picture.

Afterward, I protested to Chief Usher Rex Scouten, "What happened today? That was the sloppiest approach to meeting a head of state I've ever seen!"

Mr. Scouten just shook his head and said, "We'll have to try to explain it to them."

We straightened that out in time for the next state visit, but it was just one of a series of blunders that got on my nerves.

I wasn't feeling too well, anyway, and my appetite was poor. I was losing weight. I went to the doctor and he couldn't find anything wrong with me, so I began to wonder, is the pressure getting through to me? I began to think seriously about retiring.

In the spring of 1975 one of the ushers retired and my good friend Rex Scouten said to me, "We have an opening for usher and I hope you will take it."

Usher—that was the title I should have had for many years. I could run that office just as well as anyone else; many times I was there alone and no one thought a thing about it. There was no function I couldn't and didn't perform. From the gate, the police would phone me to clear someone for admittance to the White House, and if I had any doubts, I'd tell them to hold the person until I checked further. They relied on my judgment.

Then I had all my regular work as doorman—the foot and leg work. No usher moved from his chair if he could help it.

All those years I carried big responsibilities, at a salary I couldn't live on, let alone send my children to college. Like nearly every member of the White House household staff, except for the ushers and head chef, I'd had to take every bit of overtime work I could get at the White House plus moonlight on the outside, barbering, landscaping, whatever I could find time to do.

That has always seemed wrong to me. With the kind of spotless, beyond-reproach character we had to maintain—we couldn't even get a traffic violation without worrying about our jobs—and the high security clearance we'd earned, there was no reason in the world we shouldn't earn enough so we wouldn't have to go out and work somewhere else to make ends meet.

The people who work at the White House are trained and trusted; they know their work and do it. There is no hanging around. We never slack or shirk our work because we are happy to do it. We know that whatever we do is going to affect the family upstairs. We dearly love our work, and whoever approves the White House budget, in the Congress or wherever, must know that, and they take advantage of us.

For many years, most people had called me an usher —the police, Secret Service, the workers in the Social Office, including my dear friend Betty Hogue—everybody but the ushers themselves. Now I had the chance to take that title, officially. I was tempted.

But I knew better. I needed to slow down and relax, to work in my garden, and enjoy my grandchildren. The offer came too late but I was proud to be the first black man in the history of the White House to be offered the post of usher.

I left the White House in June 1975 and went to my country home in Pleasantville, New Jersey, for the summer. It would be the longest vacation I'd ever had.

In July, Terry O. Donnell, an aide to President Ford, called me in New Jersey to ask me to come to the Oval Office the next Tuesday at one P.M. with my whole family for picture-taking. The following week, the President asked Rex Scouten to take my family upstairs and show them all over the White House family quarters.

Two weeks later my colleagues on the White House staff gave me a farewell party in the White House movie theater. Close to two hundred people came— friends from the West Wing and the Executive Office Building as well as my co-workers in the East Wing.

President Ford himself gave me a Certificate of Commendation for my good work at the White House. I had come a long long way since those early days when I sat on a bench in the hall outside the Usher's Office.

Then Chief Usher Rex Scouten came forward to present me with a silver tray, which my White House friends had pitched in to buy for me. He spoke about me, but I can't remember anything he said, my emotions were too heavy. All I could think of was: this is it, I'm out. It felt like the end of the world. How could my White House life end so abruptly?

I couldn't respond with a single word to Rex Scouten, my wonderful friend. We had shared so much—not only our devotion to the White House. We had many deep conversations together; neither of us cared for gossip or small talk. We were both serious family men, that was something important we had in common, and we'd talk about our loved ones. Both of us read the newspapers and we'd discuss what was happening, how it related to the past and where it might lead to in the future.

I worked hard to convince Mr. Scouten to take the job of Chief Usher after Mr. West retired. I pressured him and I persuaded others to prevail upon him because I knew he was the perfect man for that position. He didn't really want the job for himself—it is a tremendous responsibility, one that he was willing to accept and he knew he could do it, but he was not eager for it. I told him he had to do it for the good of the White House.

I have never in my life known Mr. Scouten to be rude to anyone, and there were people he should have been rude to, but they didn't stay long at the White House.

He is fair and straight. I could go to him with any sug-
gestion, and he'd always listen. He'd let me go ahead
and try out my idea, and it would work.

I was lucky to work under three outstanding chief
ushers. Mr. Crim was of the old school, pretty conservative about making changes, but he let me begin to
make something more out of my job than the routine
duties of a doorman. Then to Mr. West I give all the
credit for his liberal attitude. He allowed me to make
my job important.

The chief ushers set the example for everyone on the
White House staff. They must be considerate to all of us
who work there, very flexible to handle the unexpected, and efficient, so that everything runs smoothly
for the presidents and their families.

As I stood holding that silver tray, inscribed with my
initials and my dates of service at the White House,
memories flooded over me of each President in that
beautiful theater, starting with Dwight D. Eisenhower,
who loved his westerns so much that I hated to bring
the phone to his seat.

Each man was so different, yet I saw them as a group,
uniquely privileged, uniquely burdened.

Each new President I've known started out in his
office with a different style. Some felt their way cau-
tiously, while others, like President Kennedy, relished
the glamour and importance of their new job. The only
one of them who grasped the staggering burden he'd
have to bear right from the very first day was President
Johnson.

But within a few short weeks after the inauguration,
exactly the same thing had happened to each of the
others: he'd be struck by the idea "Okay, here I am the

President; the whole weight is on *me*. The whole world is looking to *me* for answers." It became his constant thought to find ways to soothe the minds and hearts of all the people. He realized his time was no longer his own, but must be used for the good of the country. President Ford couldn't afford to waste the time to toast his own English muffins.

I watched each President change as his term of office wore on. The job transforms a man; his eyes become preoccupied, his shoulders bow, he glances at his watch every few minutes from the moment he awakes until he goes to sleep.

Every President wants to do his best, to go down in history as a great leader. But no matter what he does, every President is brutally criticized, often unfairly. President Eisenhower handled the attacks the best of any, I thought. He'd never lower himself to answer. I heard him say to Mrs. Eisenhower when she begged him to fight back, "I know I am not that person"—he meant the person described by his attackers.

The political attacks, the crushing responsibilities, the constant awareness of the danger of physical assassination—no wonder the job takes its toll on every President. I could see it in their faces as they aged before their time.

As the Presidents changed, and were worn down, so was I. Each President affected me deeply. I suffered with every one of them. I followed their problems in the news so that I could console them when things went wrong. I had created rapport between us; in my heart they became my family, my charges.

My job gave me greater access to the presidents than anyone else had in the White House except for the

valets. I saw them first thing in the morning, and at
night just before they went to bed. It was a very rich
experience to be that close to them; I saw they weren't
perfect, yet my respect and affection carried through
from one day to the next. As doorman I was the first to
greet a newly inaugurated President and the last to say
goodbye when he left.

Like so many of my colleagues, I became extremely
protective of every President. My own convenience no
longer mattered to me as it had before I came to work
at the White House. Working overtime without pay
when the First Family needed me seemed natural; I
didn't care about the time.

I'd had special training and security clearance that
belonged to my job alone, so no one could take my
place except another doorman, if there was one on
duty. That is true of all of us on the White House staff;
there are no substitutions, no doubling in brass. No one
moves into another man's job.

Never did I rush to leave the White House at the end
of my shift. I thought of how the President would still
be there, whenever I left. I could go home; he was still
working. He could never leave *his* job behind.

The sacrifices I made seemed small, compared to the
cares of a President.

After Mr. Scouten gave me the tray, everyone
crowded around me. Many of my friends had tears in
their eyes, because I was leaving and had been a help
to them. One man with whom I'd had differences made
a point to come and tell me how much he'd liked working with me and would miss me.

Walking out of the White House that day was one

of the toughest things I've ever had to do in my life.

I had a hard time adjusting to retirement that summer. My weight dropped dangerously, to only 130 pounds; I couldn't eat. I missed the White House too much.

After I returned to Washington in September, Mr. Scouten phoned me and said, "Bruce, we really need you over here—can you help us out with our social functions?"

I told him I'd be glad to.

I came back to the White House to help with another arrival ceremony. President Ford was waiting in the Diplomatic Reception Room and he looked across the room and saw me.

"Here's Mr. Bruce!" he hailed. He came over to where I was standing, pumped my hand, and clapped me on the back.

"I'm delighted you're here, Bruce! We feel secure when you are here."

So I said, "Well, Mr. President, you told me to come back and here I am!"

"We love to have you," the President told me. After that, whenever he saw me, he gave me a big welcome. That meant a lot, to be recognized like that by the President, after my retirement. I served all of the social functions until President Ford left office. It was said that in my years at the White House I had greeted more guests than any of the thirty-six men who had been President of the United States.

I look back on my years at the White House as the fruit of the dream that my father and I shared. His faith in me made me feel I could go far and I did. My father gave me his love of history. That is why I was always so fascinated to be close to the presidents as they made their decisions, and then to watch the consequences of those decisions unfold. I always tried to predict where the presidents' policies would take us—many times I was right.

And let me tell you something, to the very last day I worked there it was the same way. The day I left, the White House was just as exciting to me as the day that I went in there.

Right up to the last day, I took nothing for granted— nothing! I had privileges but I didn't abuse them. I was as serious in my work as when I first began—only I knew more about it. I never got careless just because I had been there a long time.

Some jobs you just don't want to go to. But each time I got up in the morning and headed out for the White House; I wanted to go. I knew something was going to happen that day that hadn't happened before and I wanted to be a part of it. Even when I'd go on vacation I hated to leave—I knew I'd be missing something important. So my twenty-five years at the White House were the happiest work years and the most interesting of my life.

# INDEX

# INDEX